Communitarian Ethics

Communitarian Ethics

Later Writings of Walter G. Muelder

J. Philip Wogaman

Editor

Foreword by Thomas J. Gallen

Library of Congress Control Number: 2007933139

ISBN 0-9711146-3-3
EAN 9780971114630

PUBLISHER
The Preachers' Aid Society of New England
in cooperation with BW Press,
PO Box 458, North Berwick, ME 03906

PRINTED IN THE UNITED STATES OF AMERICA

Contents

Foreword

One spring morning several years ago, I called Walter Muelder to tell him that he was to receive the "Golden Cane Award" of the New England Annual Conference of the United Methodist Church. The award is given to the oldest living pastor in New England United Methodism with the longest period of continuous service to the church. His response: "Well, that's wonderful! It's amazing how many honors come your way if you just get up one more morning than the next person!" This was pure Muelder—appreciative, but keeping everything in perspective!

Several months later the Preachers' Aid Society sent a car to bring Walter and his close friend Paul Deats to the annual clergy luncheon preceding our New England Annual Conference session. In a barely audible voice, and to a hushed and respectful room filled with those he had mentored and now considered as colleagues, Walter shared his last admonitions, urging our pastors to stay on the cutting edge of the social movements in our society and the world. The next day, at our request, he put his comments in writing and mailed them. The day after that (Saturday) he passed away—and we received the full text of his comments on Monday morning. They are included in this small volume.

Personally, it was my privilege to be Walter and Martha's pastor for three years in Newton, Massachusetts. As often as not during those years, he was my pastor. One Sunday morning is as clear to me as if it were yesterday. It was the Sunday after Christmas, and I was unexpectedly embarking on my mid-life crisis. I told the congregation just before the last hymn that I would be taking several months off to ponder life after divorce, two immediate family deaths and sundry other personal "issues." No one knew this was coming. As the last verse of the last hymn was being sung, Walter quietly made his way to the front of the sanctuary and stood alongside me for the benediction. He asked to speak to the congregation and shared his personal brief concern before we closed. "Thom, we respect your ministry among us and your decision to take this personal time. I know I speak for the many other clergy in this congregation when I say that there are enough of us here to share in caring for the needs of this congregation while you are gone. We will care for this church while you are away, and we look forward to celebrating your return soon." And they did.

Walter and Martha Muelder gave decades of devotion to the Newton Center United Methodist Church and its successor congregation. They were an integral part of its leadership and rarely missed a Sunday worship service. For many years, Walter was a powerful voice on the Board of Trustees and helped create a major and innovative endowment for use in the church and local community, and to benefit Boston University School of Theology students. In addition to being one of the great theological minds of our generation, his was a wonderfully compassionate spirit.

In his essay on "Communitarian Christian Ethics," which closes the volume edited by Paul Deats, Jr., *Toward a Discipline of Social Ethics: Essays in Honor of Walter George Muelder* (Boston University Press, 1972), Walter affirms the deep pietistic traditions that shaped his life and ministry. He makes this autobiographical observation of the impact of the Christian mystical writers on his life:

"Devotional piety and reading great mystics has helped keep alive the first-hand religious experience of the 'amateur'; it has constantly corrected tendencies toward second-hand 'professionalism.' I often have a mild mystical experience in the midst of corporate worship." (page 298)

L. Harold DeWolf captures this side of Dean Muelder beautifully: "Less well known to the general public are his personal piety and self-discipline. He has always been ready to make lonely decisions and to stand by them with courage. His personal life is a model of probity. Moreover, when he preached in chapel or led the devotions of smaller groups, it was evident that he was a man of prayer steeped in the great traditions of Christian devotion."

Walter Muelder was at once a profound philosopher/sociologist/theologian and a deeply caring pastor in and to the academic and church community. He had a vision for a worldwide social ethic that is sorely needed as we begin our grim (thus far) pilgrimage into the 21st century: "I still envision an ecumenical movement—Protestant, Orthodox, Roman Catholic—that will give transnationally a unified moral witness." I suspect that in today's world his vision would include the mythic roots of many other religious traditions as well.

We are indebted to many folks who helped bring about this volume. Seth Asare made known Walter's later writings for The United Methodist Church of Newton. Stephen Swecker, editor of *The Progressive Christian*, coordinated the production. J. Philip Wogaman, one of Walter's most distinguished students and prominent ethicist in his own right, provided the editorial work and commentary. And the Muelder families gave great encouragement and assistance.

The Preachers' Aid Society of New England is honored to be a part of bringing you this "post-script" from the heart and spirit of Dean Walter G. Muelder, our mentor, colleague and friend.

– THOMAS J. GALLEN
Executive Director
Preachers' Aid Society of New England

Communitarian Ethics

Introduction

The essays collected in this small volume are but a fragment of the legacy left by Walter George Muelder. One of the 20th century's greatest ethicists, Muelder taught generations of graduate students at Boston University School of Theology during his 27-year tenure as Dean and Professor of Social Ethics. That tenure ended in 1972, but he continued teaching at Berea College and Garrett-Evangelical Theological Seminary before returning to Boston to resume part-time teaching until close to the end of his life on June 12, 2004. His written legacy is impressive with ten books, written or edited, two dozen chapters in books edited by others, and 150 or so published articles. But the living legacy of hundreds of students and his incalculable intellectual and moral contributions to his Methodist denomination and the broader ecumenical movement may be more significant, even, than those writings.

These essays are the work of an extraordinarily productive mind. Even more remarkably, many of them were written *after Dean Muelder had turned 94!* So much for the inevitable deterioration of the human mind! One of the short writings in this collection was written only three days before Muelder died at the age of 97.

Most of the writings presented here are topical. They address a few of the issues facing humanity in the early years of the 21st century. While he was deeply grounded in philosophy and theology, Muelder did not disdain speaking and writing on contemporary problems. Such writing may appear to be ephemeral, but it is precisely as an ethicist confronts the problems of the moment that he or she illuminates the enduring values and insights of serious thought. Put differently, without dealing with actual problems in some detail, theology and ethics can be reduced to irrelevant abstraction. On the other hand, as a great ethicist like Walter Muelder struggles with the details of contemporary life, it is helpful to know more about his or her deeper convictions and methods.

So, where was Muelder "coming from"? I wish to highlight five main points.[1]

I. Philosophical and Theological Personalism

Muelder was, first, a product of and contributor to "Boston Personalism." Associated especially with turn-of-the-century philosopher Borden Parker Bowne, Muelder's own teachers Edgar S. Brightman and Albert C. Knudsen, and Muelder's contemporary L. Harold DeWolf, Personalism has blended philosophical metaphysics and Christian theism. The ultimate principle of reality is personal. God is person—incomparably more than human, of course. But, and the point must be underscored, God is *no less* than human. Human beings are also persons. The capacity to think and to love is the spark of the divine in each of us, enabling us to be in relationship with God and to live in accordance with God's deep purposes. Tendencies toward excessive individualism in earlier personalism found correction in Muelder's and DeWolf's communitarian emphasis. To be a person is to be in community. Apart from community, we are depersonalized.

---

1. It is, of course, well beyond the scope of this introduction to provide a full account of Muelder's contributions to ethics. Two of his books are particularly valuable as comprehensive expositions of his thought: *Foundations of the Responsible Society* (Nashville: Abingdon Press, 1959) and *Moral Law in Christian Social Ethics* (Richmond, Va.: John Knox Press, 1966). A festschrift in his honor, *Toward A Discipline of Social Ethics: Essays in Honor of Walter George Muelder* (Boston: Boston Univ. Press, 1972) includes an appreciative interpretation of his thought by Paul Deats, Jr., the book's editor, and C. Eric Lincoln, along with Muelder's own thoughtful response. A collection of his essays, drawn from 40 years of writing, is contained in *Walter G. Muelder, The Ethical Edge of Christian Theology: Forty Years of Communitarian Personalism* (NY and Toronto: The Edwin Mellen Press, 1983). And one of my favorites among his shorter books is *In Every Place A Voice* (Cincinnati: Woman's Division of Christian Service of the Methodist Church, 1957).

I recall a memorable response by Muelder in one of his graduate seminars. We were discussing the effects of poverty and malnutrition on the spiritual development of children. A somewhat pietistic student asked whether a child under such conditions could not still experience the love of God. That, declared Muelder, "is pure sentimental slop."

Because of his grasp of the importance of community, Muelder became a pioneer in the development of social ethics as an academic discipline. To him, this was a direct outgrowth of the personalistic tradition in philosophy and theology by which he was nurtured intellectually, although he carried this much further than his own teachers. He made substantial use of the "moral laws" of Edgar S. Brightman, but joined L. Harold DeWolf in providing them with distinctly communitarian and theological dimensions. The broad outline is very simple: we are persons in community—a community cannot exist without persons who, as individuals, think and value. But such persons are unthinkable apart from their existence in community. And both persons and community gain their ultimate meaning from their relationship with God.

This broad, simple outline is carefully articulated and defended by Muelder and others of that tradition. Because of its philsophical origins in 19th century Germany and its 20th century American developments as a philosophical tradition, Muelder and others are sometimes misunderstood as neglecting theology. Muelder was, in fact, an unusually gifted philosopher, more complete, more rigorous than so many philosophers in recent years who have neglected metaphysics while concentrating primarily on linguistic analysis. But, perhaps precisely because of his personalistic metaphysics, Muelder has been able to blend his philosophical position with serious Christian theological commitments almost seamlessly. It is arguable that Muelder and other Boston personalists did not fully grasp the possibilities of the so-called "neo-orthodox" position of the Barthians and others. But the latter more seriously neglected the resources of philosophy, the social sciences, and other secular disciplines of learning. When such resources are disdained, the relationship between theology and the factual world in which moral judgments must be made is largely left to intuition. But intuition can so easily mislead us; worse, it can be captive to cultural values and biases that are remote from Christian faith. That may be especially the case when moral judgments are made about groups that are very different from our own.

II. The Interdisciplinary Character of Christian Ethics

For such reasons, and because of his rigorous attention to epistemological questions, Muelder saw Christian ethics as a multi-disciplinary enterprise. It could be described as the discipline that attends to the connections among the disciplines that are relevant to moral life. To be an ethicist is not to be an authority on Bible, historical and systematic theology, world religions, economics, political science, anthropology, sociology, psychology and the physical sciences. It is to try to be an expert on how the insights of these and other fields are to be related to one another in the task at hand. To do this well, an ethicist must be well-grounded in the history of ethics and in the unique resources of the discipline.

The task of ethics, thus, is never finished. Muelder's philosophical mentor, Edgar S. Brightman, understood truth to be disclosed through what he called "comprehensive coherence." That is, our grasp of reality is contained in the coherence of sources of knowledge. "Comprehensive coherence" is thus more than simple non-contradiction, although contradictions must somehow be resolved if our understandings are to become coherent. Muelder carried this a step further by his insight that coherence is never complete—we never have the whole truth. So he wrote and spoke of ethics as "emergent coherence." Moral truth is always in the process of emerging. New discoveries and insights in any of the relevant disciplines affect our understanding of the others and of how moral issues are to be framed and addressed.

This view of the ethical enterprise has consequences. One of these is recognition that any ethicist is likely to be better at some of the relevant disciplines than others. Muelder himself, trained theologically and philosophically, was especially interested in sociology and economics. Some of his earliest recognized work was sociological.[2] His interests in economics were prompted in part by early commitments to the labor movement and socialism. While he later concluded that a mixed economy was preferable to pure socialism, his later *Religion and Economic Responsibility*[3] broadened and deepened those moral commitments.

A related consequence of "emergent coherence" was especially appreciated by generations of Muelder's doctoral students in ethics. That was his encouragement to pursue their own unique interests. So one student might be most interested in political science, another in ecumenical ethics, another in economics, another in race relations. All were expected to master a common core of material, such as the history of ethics, and the expectation was rigorously applied. But Muelder understood that different ones of us would make our contributions at different points. His approach to doctoral mentoring was thus quite unlike that of some doctoral advisors who have seemed more interested in attracting disciples whose work would contribute directly to the advisors' own publishing program. Muelder had a deep respect for the intellectual independence of others and how that, properly nurtured, might enhance the "emergent coherence" of the whole ethical enterprise.

A less direct, but no less important consequence, was to engender a spirit of intellectual humility. None of us can know everything; indeed, in the long, long run, none of us know very much. We must continue to grow, intellectually and spiritually, welcoming new knowledge and insight wherever they are to be found. Superficially, but only superficially, this attitude might appear to be a form of skepticism: if we cannot be sure of final truth, how can we be sure of anything? But Muelder's view was far from that kind of relativism. "Emergent coherence" is in fact a quite rigorous test of truth. To put it in ordinary speech, does a viewpoint "make sense" in light of everything else we know? And, if a new insight "makes sense," is it not all the more likely that we will gain still more new insights? We may have to change our views quite radi-

---

2. See, for example, his 1945 essay "From Sect to Church," reprinted in J. Milton Yinger, *Religion, Society, and the Individual: An Introduction to the Sociology of Religion* (New York: Macmillan, 1957), pp. 480-488.

3. New York: Scribner's, 1953.

cally, but that is not at all the same thing as saying that we cannot depend upon any perceptions of reality.

More to the point of the moral life, we are deeply committed to the good as we are given to understand it—prepared to exchange it only for a greater good, but not for no good at all. I vividly recall an intense conversation with Walter Muelder and Paul Deats during which Muelder—already an old man—changed a view he had held for a very long time on a subject vexing the churches. It was a subject on which I had also changed my mind! When churches function in this spirit they are able to grow, not by being skeptical of all truth, but by seeking to come ever closer to the mind of God.

III. The Engagement of Church and Society

Muelder was a student of the social teaching of Christian churches throughout his professional life. One of his most important books, *Methodism and Society in the Twentieth Century*,[4] remains the best introduction to the social teaching and practices of this denomination from 1908 to the volume's publication in 1961. Indeed, that volume's insights are strikingly relevant to other mainline denominations as well as Methodism. He writes,

"The social witness of Methodism is full of lights and shadows. Its history is a fluctuating and pulsating movement determined by its own growing understanding of its gospel and mission and by the tempestuous events of America's developing civilization. Its tempo varies from region to region and from one annual conference to another.... All in all, as the succeeding pages will show, The Methodist Church has struggled to save the world beyond its doors and the worldliness which occupies its pews and sometimes designs its policies. This book tells the story of Christian social conscience in the present century."[5]

As one of the writings in the present volume demonstrates, Muelder was conscious of the importance of the formal pronouncements of church bodies. His insights into their possibilities

---

4. Nashville: Abingdon Press, 1961.
5. *Ibid*, pp. 36-37

and limitations are well worth thoughtful consideration by all who are called upon to formulate and vote upon such statements.

At the same time, he understood that the church teaches by what it does as well as by what it says. In this respect, he was greatly influenced by Ernst Troeltsch's *The Social Teaching of the Christian Churches.*[6] Troeltsch had observed that even a church's basic form of institutional organization is implicitly a part of its social teaching.

Throughout his adult life, Muelder was actively committed to the church. While he was an ordained Methodist (later, United Methodist) minister, most of his career was in academic settings and not in the pulpit. So his local church participation was, essentially though not officially, as a layperson. The tribute later in this volume by one of his pastors illustrates that his local church involvements were not perfunctory, nor was his participation in regional and denominational bodies. In all of his various church contexts he was especially concerned that the church's moral teaching should be deeply grounded in the shared faith and that it not be in conflict with its practice.

IV. Ecumenical Commitments

Muelder was not a participant in the formative ecumenical conferences, such as the Oxford Conference of 1937 and the 1st Assembly of the World Council of Churches (WCC) of 1948, but he quickly committed himself to the ecumenical movement.[7] He found the 1948 WCC concept of the "Responsible Society" to be extraordinarily insightful, to the point that two of his most important books were greatly influenced by it.[8] A smaller third book, *In Every Place A Voice*, was based on the call of that 1948 Assembly

---

6. New York: Macmillan, 1931. Translated from the 1911 German edition by Olive Wyon. Muelder's doctoral students were required to plough their way through that formidable two-volume work.

7. In an intellectual autobiography, Muelder remarks that "I am grateful to have had the privilege of living and working in the era of the ecumenical movement." Muelder, "Communitarian Christian Ethics: A Personal Statement and a Response," in Deats, ed., *Toward a Discipline of Social Ethics*, p. 318.

8. *Religion and Economic Responsibility* and *Foundations of the Responsible Society.*

that "We have to make of the Church in every place a voice for those who have no voice, and a home where every man will be at home." In such writings, Muelder sought to flesh out such themes, lest they not become empty platitudes. As a teacher and writer, he encouraged others to commit themselves to an ecumenical vision. In this, he was also an extraordinary model, with a wide variety of ecumenical involvements from local to global. He worked actively in the Massachusetts Council of Churches, the Department of the Church and Economic Life and the Division of Christian Life and Work of the National Council of Churches. He was a delegate to the WCC Conference on Faith and Order (Lund, 1952), he taught at the WCC's Ecumenical Institute in Switzerland, served as consultant to the Evanston Assembly of the WCC (1954), was a delegate to the New Delhi Assembly (1961), the WCC Conference on Church and Society (1962) and the Uppsala Assembly (1968). He had served as co-chair of the WCC Commission on Cooperation of Men and Women in the Church and as chair of the WCC Commission on Institutionalism.[9]

This does not mean that he lacked commitment to his own denomination. He was a lifelong Methodist, son of a Methodist minister, ordained an elder in that denomination, frequently consulted by its leaders and served as a General Conference delegate. But he took pride in the contributions Methodism had made to the ecumenical movement from the very beginning and saw Methodism's ecumenical commitments to be an integral part of its denominational meaning.

Most of his ecumenical commitments were expressed in the relationships of mainline denominations with one another, and to the work of its leading theologians of which he came to be one. But his ecumenical horizon was not limited even to Christianity. He sought out relationships with persons of other faiths, even appointing a leading Hindu to the School of Theology faculty.[10]

---

9. See Paul K. Deats, Jr. and C. Eric Lincoln, "Walter G. Muelder: An Appreciation," in Deats, ed., *Toward a Discipline of Social Ethics*, p. 15-16.

10. The distinguished Hindu scholar, Amiya Chakravarty, had been an intimate of the leaders of the Indian independence movement, including Gandhi and Nehru, and had served as secretary to the Bengali poet Tagore. Muelder was criticized for this appointment by some within the denomination who lacked his vision, but he refused to abandon that

V. World Community and World Peace

Of a piece with this was his deep commitment to the United Nations, treating this body as the most promising instrument for the achievement of world community. With respect to that, he was fond of saying that "mankind[11] is the unit of cooperation." To him, our commitment to global society must be ethically prior to our allegiance to any nation. Thus, Muelder writes that Christ, as Lord over the world, "has given as the goal the creation in history of a barrierless community for the whole of mankind. Each man has a vocation to serve to bring this community into existence."[12]

Global community was not to be regarded, however, simply as an ideal; it is already a present reality, though imperfectly realized. Practically, this is an acknowledgment of a rich fabric of existing cultural, economic, and political interrelationships spanning the globe. Morally, it recognizes God's prior relationship with every person and the moral claim of each upon all. He welcomed the emergence of the United Nations, born out of the catastrophic World War II, as the most promising institutional basis for a new world order. Writing in 1959, he acknowledged that some kinds of international disputes, of a more regional character, need not involve the UN. But the world body "must be made more effective to handle major transportation and natural resource matters." Written prior to the end of the Cold War around 1990, these words anticipated a good deal of effective international cooperation in various non-military spheres. But Muelder was especially concerned about the dangers of nuclear conflict and the need for the United Nations to confront them:

"...if the United Nations is to be truly effective, it must in the crucial areas affecting world-wide interests be given a monopoly of jurisdiction and power. It must have a monopoly on certain

---

interreligious commitment.

11. Like virtually all theologians of the period, Muelder used generic male language. His commitments to gender inclusiveness were real, however, and often expressed. During the 1950s he led an important ecumenical program on the Status and Role of Women, opening up issues that many—perhaps most—ecumenical leaders would just as soon not have discussed.

12. *Moral Law in Christian Social Ethics*, p. 165.

kinds of force, and this means the transference of the corresponding aspect of national sovereignty to the authority of the world government.... The United Nations must be given the power to guarantee a stable equilibrium definable as peace. On the negative side this means that nation-states must surrender all nuclear bomb test privileges to the UN.... We are led to conclude that negatively speaking the church must completely repudiate the use and testing of H-bombs and that positively speaking all such power must be assigned to the UN."[13]

Was Muelder a pacifist? He frequently characterized himself in that way. In his 1950 essay, "Why I Believe in Pacifism," Muelder writes that "Faith in God's creative and redemptive power despite personal death is the ultimate rootage of the pacifist way of life. The pacifist lives as he does because Jesus lived and died as he did."[14] Later, he would write that "recourse to modern warfare is an appeal to incalculable evil," adding, "the church cannot bear a clear testimony against war today without repudiating the H-bomb. It cannot today reject the bomb without repudiating war itself."[15]

Muelder's commitments to pacifism did not seem to rule out responsible uses of police power within a national community nor responsible uses of power by the world community, with its hoped-for monopoly of the power needed to protect the international order. Clearly, Muelder rejected modern warfare between and among nation-states and any uses of nuclear weaponry. And he embraced the "pacifist way of life" as the spiritual commitment of a Christian believer. While much impressed by the possibilities and successes of non-violent resistance, as embodied in the campaigns of M. K. Gandhi and Martin Luther King, Jr., he did not think of pacifism in simply pragmatic terms. "*Agape* ethics as nonviolent action must be viewed not simply as a method but as a way of life."[16]

---

13. *Foundations of the Responsible Society*, pp. 278-280.

14. Quoted by Joseph D. Stamey, "The Disciplines of Power: The Necessity and Limits of Coercion," in Deats, ed., *Toward a Discipline of Social Ethics*, p. 162.

15. *Foundations of the Responsible Society*, pp. 263, 264.

16. Muelder, "Communitarian Christian Ethics," in Deats, ed., *Toward a Discipline of Social Ethics*, p. 315.

The Unity of Theory and Practice

Muelder was therefore committed to "the personalistic rubric of the concrete unity of theory and practice."[17] A purely abstract ethics will not do. It is a practical discipline; it must permeate one's whole life and find expression in action. Occasionally students at Boston University questioned whether Muelder himself was active enough. Such questioning overlooked a very important point: As leader of the School of Theology, Muelder understood that that institution itself embodied "practice" of the utmost importance. Concluding his essay on "Communitarian Christian Ethics," he writes:

"The university is itself a vital part of the world's social order and therefore it is the time and place for the embodiment of the responsible society. Here conflict, conflict resolution, and reconciliation should be the expected order of the day. The university is chartered for dissent—for responsible dissent. No institution in society is in a better position to recognize that all previous foundations of truth and art, of virtue and piety are historically conditioned and that its present efforts are also under judgment. No community has a better opportunity to prepare leaders through living in tomorrow's world by anticipation. No anticipation of the future carries with it a greater obligation to be responsive and responsible than the day-by-day experiences of the academic community."[18]

That, doubtless, is his own vocational affirmation. It represents the sphere of action to which he must be committed personally. Was he, in and through this vocational commitment, able to fulfill the lofty understanding of what a university can be?

Despite failures and imperfections, the Boston University School of Theology throughout his 27 years of leadership had an extraordinary record for inspiring and equipping leaders for social change. The best-known illustration is, of course, Dr. Martin Luther King, Jr., whose doctoral studies were at Boston University.

---

17. *Ibid.*, p. 319.
18. *Ibid.*, pp. 319-310.

Less well-known is the fact that into the 1960s half of the doctoral degrees in religious studies held by African Americans in the United States were conferred by that one university—a splendid tribute to Boston University, a shameful judgment upon the rest of American higher education. But the University's example helped lead the way for the rest of higher education in subsequent decades. Muelder recruited a faculty that included such scholar-activists as Dr. Alan Knight Chalmers, Professor of Homiletics, who was a leader in the NAACP Legal Defense Fund and who, during my own years at BU, was in and out of the South in constant support of racial justice. Prof. L. Harold DeWolf, who served as King's doctoral studies advisor, made constant contributions to the Civil Rights Movement. Prof. Paul Deats was deeply engaged in social justice causes in New England. And the list could go on.

And as the list goes on, it includes large numbers of students who, with that heritage, were to become social action leaders all over the country and around the world. So Muelder's own decision to focus his activist energies upon this institution proved to be quite productive.[19]

–JPW

---

19. As a personal note, I found the insights of this great teacher very helpful in eight years of preaching to a President of the United States and other national leaders.

A Personal Appreciation

Everybody who studied with or was otherwise influenced by Walter Muelder can be grateful for the life and work of this great teacher. One of those, the Rev. Dr. Seth Ahene Asare, was responsible for collecting most of the writings in Part I of this book. He explains here how this developed out of his personal relationship with and appreciation for Dr. Muelder.

In 1989 I was appointed E. Stanley Jones Professor of Evangelism at Boston University. At that time, Professor Walter Muelder was still teaching courses at the school, and I was asked to share an office with him. During the few months that we shared a common space, I came to know and admire this spiritual and academic giant. Beyond the legacy of his name and reputation, I had the privilege of knowing the man. He was generous in his affirmations and encouragement. He had a way of making me think through my statements by providing me with the rich background and history of various situations.

In 1993, I was appointed to Newton (Massachusetts) United Methodist Church to serve as Dr. Muelder's pastor. My first thought was, "How on earth am I going to preach every Sunday with Dr. Muelder sitting in the pew?" Characteristically, Dr. Muelder took the initiative to make me feel at ease. Martha and Walter invited us to stay at their home when the parsonage was not ready. My family decided not to impose on them but chose instead to spend Sunday afternoons with the Muelders. My children still remember some of the games we played at their Oxford Street home.

Martha and Walter were a great support to the ministry of my family in Newton. I always knew that I could go to Dr. Muelder and seek counsel and he would give me an honest answer. I shared some of my ideas on church renewal with him. He was always ready to listen and give me some of his own ideas. I have to say that he never scolded me for not doing everything he suggested (there must have been a few times)! Our meetings ended with the two of us holding hands and spending time in prayer. The depth of his faith was always apparent in his prayers.

Dr. Muelder was a faithful member of the church community. He was in church every Sunday and would read all the lectionary passages for the day . He then would turn to each of the hymns in the bulletin as a way of preparing himself for the service. He never wanted to be the center of what was happening in the church, and he allowed the democratic process to take its course.

After his beloved Martha died, Walter and I had several conversations about what would happen when his time came. He went so far as to write instructions on what should be done. So you can imagine my anxiety when I was told that the bishop was assigning me to another church. I spoke to Dr. Muelder briefly about the move, but we did not discuss the directives he had given….

To say that Dr. Muelder was always reading and learning is an understatement. Each time he spoke, be it from the pulpit, at Men's Breakfast or at a church meeting, we listened in awe to the profound words of wisdom he had to offer. He kept abreast of social issues in the church, the state, the nation, and on the international scene. (Following are) a few of the articles that he wrote as a member of the church community. I had invited Dr. Muelder to share some ideas in writing with us in the hopes of provoking discussion within the congregation. These articles were written either for our church newsletter, as a sermon or for discussion.

Dr. Muelder was consistent in his utterances on non-violence throughout his life. He was an exceptionally good listener when it came to the views of others. However, wars and notions of "just war theories" did not agree with the "beloved community" which he saw as God's directive for the people of God. The following articles (include) some of Dr. Muelder's thoughts on a wide range of topics. From world hunger to genetic engineering to Afghanistan and Iraq, Dr. Muelder's convictions and faith are apparent in his approach to the issues facing our world today.

– SETH AHENE ASARE

Editor's Note: Two additional short writings by Walter Muelder have been selected to round out this collection of the work of his last three years, further illustrating how his incisive mind engaged the issues of the day. Brief editorial commentaries introduce each of the writings collected here in order to help provide context.

Communitarian Ethics

Part I

Final Writings of a Great
Teacher of Ethics

The Meaning of Nonviolence

While most of Dr. Muelder's career was spent as a theological educator and not as a local church pastor, he was occasionally called upon to preach in various settings. The following is the transcript of a sermon he preached on Martin Luther King Sunday, January 16, 2000. It was delivered at the United Methodist Church of Newton, where he was for many years a faithful participant and where Dr. Asare was his pastor. At the time, Muelder was 92 years old, and one notices brief acknowledgment that this might be "my possible final personal witness to you." The sermon is both a tribute to Dr. Martin Luther King, Jr., and a reaffirmation of Dr. Muelder's own long-standing pacifist commitments.

Muelder here takes justifiable pride in his own influence upon the great civil rights leader, while noting that "Martin, like all of us, was a flawed human being." The reference to King's borrowing a Fosdick sermon may also be an oblique comment on revelations that King had done some plagiarizing in his academic career, including his Boston University doctoral dissertation. The bulk of the sermon, however, is his summary of five principles of non-violent resistance. As he lays these out, with great clarity, one can sense the kind of influence Muelder had upon King himself. **–JPW**

I appreciate Pastor Asare's invitation to preach on the Sunday prior to the national recognition of Martin Luther King, Jr.

The root meaning of nonviolence is clear, simple and central in the Christian ethic, and inescapable. The symbol of nonviolence hangs before us, the cross of Jesus, the Savior. When we embrace nonviolence, we accept sacrificial love and compassion as our way of life. As Hosea, the prophet of forgiveness, said, we seek to do justly, to love mercy and to walk humbly before God. We need these virtues when we truly worship before the cross.

While I am delivering this sermon, 35 wars are raging around the world. Nonviolence is not a pacifist strategy to resolve all these conflicts. They have many causes, and appropriate solutions for each must be found. Nonviolence provides hope; despair fuels greater violence. The struggles for justice lack an essential ingredient when they lack what nonviolence affirms.

Tomorrow is the anniversary to celebrate the life and work of Dr. King and the need to finish the civil rights struggle in race relations. Today I am presenting the philosophy and theology which King embraced 50 years ago while a 22-year-old graduate student at Boston University School of Theology. He was a graduate of Morehouse College and Crozer Theological Seminary. He was the son of a Baptist clergyman in Atlanta.

Martin, like all of us, was a flawed human being. He was not above borrowing a sermon of a great preacher when he was on trial to qualify as the assistant minister in his father's church. Thus his first public oration was borrowed from "Life is What You Make It," a published sermon by Harry Emerson Fosdick of the Riverside Church in New York. Years later, in his famous "Letter from Birmingham Jail," he cited Fosdick: "Man made laws to assure justice; but a higher law produces love." Fosdick had a continuing influence in shaping King's devotion to nonviolence. I acknowledge happily that Fosdick was one of my father's and my mentors in my formative theological years. We sang one of his great hymns here this morning ("God of Grace and God of Glory").

King writes that he made his final step in his pilgrimage to nonviolence when I was his dean. He found that influence to be two-fold: a passion for social justice that is realistic and avoids superficial optimism; and a theological grounding in the grace of God at work in both persons and community. I mention King's testimony of me not to take credit, but as my possible final personal witness to you.

In forming and grounding his commitment to nonviolence, King was also influenced by Edgar S. Brightman and L. Harold DeWolf, both Newton Methodists. Later in his campaign he was assisted by Paul Deats of the Auburndale Church and by Neil Richardson. DeWolf was a theologian who taught King after Brightman's death in 1953. DeWolf taught the Adult Bible Class in this church, as some of you can remember. King's children called him Uncle Harold and Coretta had him do a eulogy at Martin's funeral, a service which I attended.

Philosophically and theologically King's nonviolence is grounded in Personal Idealism. What does this mean? This means that each person is of intrinsic worth. Each person is sacred, being grounded in the personal creativity of God. The whole cosmos, the whole of reality is through and through personal. There is no more ultimate principle. Personality is the primary explanatory principle. All our categories are derived from analyzing personal experience. All enquiry begins in personal experience, and all hypotheses must satisfy human reason. Personalizing one's view of God is not anthropomorphic. God is not super-finite. God is all the ultimate power there is, the source of all creativity, novelty and true value—that is, of all that is true, good, sublime and beautiful.

The highest ethical principle is love. Love is threefold. Love encompasses aspiring, or erotic love; brotherly love or reciprocity in community; and compassionate or sacrificial love as sublimely symbolized in the cross of Jesus. Nonviolence is a manifestation of and a practical witness to this highest form of love which is grounded in the character of God. It also embraces the other forms of love.

I affirmed at the outset that nonviolence is not a tactic, gimmick, strategy, or passing policy. It is a "way of life," often a costly way of life. It is not a political tool you pick up and then set aside. Not all persons in the civil rights struggle have understood that nonviolence is deeper than policy.

Nevertheless, nonviolence has had notable modern historical expressions: Gandhi's struggles in South Africa and in freeing India from Britain's colonial control; Mandela's strategy of inclusiveness to overcome apartheid and his work with Archbishop Tutu in the program of truth and reconciliation; and in King's valiant civil rights movement leading to major advances in inclusiveness in transportation, voting, equality of opportunity and education. These have been applications of the inclusiveness of the principle.

As a method and a way of life, nonviolent resistance as pursued by King had five principal aspects which illuminate its meaning. They are the fruit of his Boston pilgrimage.

First, it is not a method for cowards; it does resist evil and wrongdoing. If one resorts to nonviolence because one is afraid or lacks the means of violence, one is not truly nonviolent. King quotes Gandhi that, "if cowardice is the only alternative to violence, it is better to fight." But there is always another alternative. No individual or group need submit to any wrong, nor need they resort to violence to right the wrong. There is the way of nonviolent resistance. This is the way of those who are spiritually strong. They may have to suffer. Nonviolence is not passive nonresistance. The nonviolent person is not physically resisting or aggressive toward his neighbor, but he or she is constantly seeking to persuade his violent neighbor that she/he is wrong. One is spiritually not passive, but active. One seeks to resist and overcome evil.

A second aspect of nonviolence is that it does not seek to defeat or humiliate the opponent but to win the opponent's friendship and understanding. "The nonviolent resister must often express his protest through non-cooperation or boycotts, but he/she realizes that these are not ends in themselves; they are merely means to awaken a sense of moral shame in the opponent. The end is redemption and reconciliation." We cannot control all the variables that influence contemporary conflicts. But the aftermath of nonviolence is the beloved community, while the aftermath of violence is tragic bitterness. In his famous essay on "Eternal Peace," Immanuel Kant said that a peace treaty should not contain within it the seeds of a future war. The latter was the fatal flaw of the Versailles Treaty following World War I; it opened the door of nationalism, hate and racism in Hitler's movement. Vengeance among the winners led to despair and violence in the losers.

A third aspect of the method of nonviolence is that its power is directed against forces of evil rather than the persons who happen to be doing the evil. It is the evil that the nonviolent resister seeks to defeat, not the persons victimized by the evil they do. If one is opposing racial injustice, the nonviolent actor has the vision to see that the basic tension is not between races. King said to the people of Montgomery, Alabama: "The tension in this city is not between white people and Negro people. The tension is, at bottom, between justice and injustice, between the forces of light and the forces of darkness. And if there is a victory, it will be a victory not merely for 50,000 Negroes, but a victory for justice and the forces of light. We are out to defeat injustice and not white persons who may be unjust."

A fourth point that characterizes nonviolent resistance is a willingness to accept suffering without retaliation, to accept blows from the opponent without striking back. Gandhi once said, "Rivers of blood may have to flow before we gain our freedom, but it must be our blood." The nonviolent resister is willing to accept violence if necessary, but never to inflict it. He does not seek to dodge jail. If going to jail is necessary, he enters it "as a bridegroom enters the bride's chamber." Suppose someone asks, "What is the nonviolent resister's justification for this ordeal to which he/she invites others; for this mass political action of the ancient doctrine of turning the other cheek?" The answer is found in the realization that unearned suffering is redemptive. Suffering is not sought as some magic formula. The cross is not a sign by which to conquer, as Constantine thought. Yet there are educational and transforming possibilities. King quotes Gandhi as follows: "Things of fundamental importance to people are not secured by reason alone, but have to be purchased with their suffering...Suffering is infinitely more powerful than the law of the jungle for converting the opponent and opening his ears which are otherwise shut to the voice of reason." Civil justice is noble, but, as Vatican Council II noted, it is dubious that any contemporary war can meet the criteria of a just war.

The final point concerning nonviolent resistance as interpreted by King in the civil rights struggle is that it avoids not only external physical violence but also internal violence of spirit. One not only refuses to shoot his opponent but also to hate him. At the center of nonviolence stands the principle of love. In the struggle for human dignity, the oppressed people of the world need to avoid succumbing to bitterness and hate campaigns. King, Gandhi, Mandela and others have shown practical alternatives to both hate and violence. The unity of the human family is sustained by God's covenant of love with God's creation. On earth, love breaks the downward spiral of destructive hate. Hate feeds on despair. Love turns the despair into hope. Such love is sacrificial, outgoing, redemptive. It is not a sentimental alternative to justice, but elevates justice to fulfill its vocation in building community. The vocation of the church is to teach people to love people for their own sakes.

One great temptation is to treat King and his civil rights struggle as a passing historical event. But the deeper message is that as long as the cross of Jesus is relevant to understanding the nature of God, nonviolence is relevant in social change. God is not aloof from human beings, because God's creativity is forever conditioned by the creatures God is redeeming.

In this testimony of my involvement in King's pilgrimage to nonviolence, I do not pretend that it is a full-blown social ethics of the Christian life. It has not dealt with questions like "restitution" or the role of full-disclosure in the "truth and reconciliation" program led by Archbishop Tutu and Nelson Mandela. I do, however, offer it up to God as an earnest of what I have endorsed in my ministry of teaching and administration in pursuit of the beloved community and the preparation for all in the struggle of activist resistance to social evil. ☙

WAKE-UP CALL ON GLOBAL AIDS

In this brief article, published in the Newton church's Fellowship News in February, 2001, Muelder illustrates both his continuing attention to urgent social issues and the timeliness of his data. The information conveyed here remains substantially accurate. As of the end of 2006, the UNAIDS/WHO information center concluded that some 24 million people are HIV/AIDS positive in sub-Saharan Africa. At that point in time, the agency estimated a global total of 39.5 million infected people, and that some 25 million have died of AIDS since 1981. In Africa alone, 12 million children have been orphaned by AIDS.

In developing countries some 6.8 million people needed AIDS drugs, but only 1.65 million were receiving them. Muelder's comments about the link between AIDS and breastfeeding are in accord with the latest data, although that issue is complex and in some dispute. But the mind boggles at the enormity of the AIDS problem—possibly (as the quoted view of Michael Merson suggests), the AIDS tragedy can be compared to the plague epidemic in the Middle Ages.

Echoing his long-standing view that "mankind is the unit of cooperation," Muelder comments here that "we are all bound in a single bundle of life." In this brief writing, he does not belabor the ethical implications of that, but he makes clear that HIV/AIDS cannot simply be dismissed as a result of risky and sinful behavior patterns. While commending the Gates Foundation for its work—which has become even much more involved since 2001—Muelder calls upon governments and churches to wake up. **–JPW**

For a century and more we have known that infectious diseases know no class, race or national boundaries. We are all bound in a single bundle of life. Bill Gates knows this, and with his wife, Melinda, has outspent the entire U.S. government by almost $300 million this past year to combat global health threats such as

AIDS, malaria and tuberculosis. Indeed, he gave more than a quarter of what all industrialized countries spent for the health needs of underdeveloped nations. Not that Gates should do less, but rich governments, including the United States, should be doing more.

This plea has also been made by the dean of the School of Public Health of Columbia University after he attended the XIIIth International Conference in Durban, South Africa.

Dean Allen Rosenfeld points out that, "there are now 28 million HIV-positive men, women, and children in sub-Saharan Africa, all of whom will die soon because no modern therapies are available." As many as 12 million children have been orphaned as a result of AIDS.

As *The Economist* reports, "What needed to be shouted from the rooftops was that, contrary to some popular views, AIDS is not primarily a disease of gay western men or intravenous drug injectors. It is a disease of ordinary people leading ordinary lives, except that most of them happen to live in a continent, Africa, that the rich countries find easy to ignore."

Dr. Michael Merson, dean, Yale School of Public Health, makes the magnitude of the epidemic frightfully clear as follows:

• One third of all young adults in Africa are infected with the virus (more women than men).

• 80 percent of all hospital beds are occupied by AIDS patients suffering from tuberculosis and other infectious diseases.

• The average life expectancy is 30 years.

• 28 million AIDS orphans are expected by 2010.

• The above situation results in an estimated decrease of 15 to 20 percent in Gross Domestic Production.

The dean adds that this is one of the greatest tragedies in the history of our civilization—more severe than the plague epidemic in the Middle Ages in Europe.

We must move from awareness to action. Both governmental and nongovernmental action on a massive scale are required to deal with this tragedy. On one hand, needed is equity in access to care, particularly to expensive antiretroviral drugs that improve and prolong the lives of AIDS patients. Pharmaceutical companies that make these drugs can make more donations and rich governments are offering billions of dollars in credits. However, the poorest nations need not credits but cancellation of debts, or they get ever deeper in trouble financially. Churches have been urging such debt relief.

Training in care and prevention methods is also needed. For example, breast-feeding of infants spreads the disease. Prevention can be very helpful. Prevention programs, including widespread education, with sex education in schools and use of condoms, plus social marketing and counseling, can greatly reduce the spread of AIDS. Prevention is as important in the long run as access to immediate care. About $3 billion is needed for prevention in sub-Saharan Africa; and yet, only $600 million is available to developing countries worldwide.

The churches can play a significant role in taking secrecy about AIDS transmission away and by motivating governments to take long-term preventive measures. There is no greater priority for international health and development. This crisis speaks to American international policy as to all rich governments. ⌽

Moral and Religious Issues in the Genome Project

This article, originally appearing in the Newton church paper, summarizes important issues arising from the Genome Project. Data presented here is substantially accurate, although the project has now been completed; the human genome has now been successfully mapped. Interestingly, the head of the Human Genome Project at the U. S. National Institutes of Health, Dr. Francis S. Collins, has become a major figure in the debates over science and religion, arguing persuasively that scientific methods and conclusions point toward, not away from, religious belief.

As an ethicist, Muelder devoted relatively little time to issues in bioethics. Nevertheless, this short essay reveals his questing mind and the precision with which he could identify ethical issues in a field where he was far from being an expert himself. In posing the questions, one notes that he does not offer much in the way of conclusions. Still, he is able to discern important issues ranging from the economic implications for poorer countries whose ability to make use of biological knowledge could be limited by patenting of genetic knowledge to issues of privacy and uses of genetic therapy. His reference to eugenics calls to mind the earlier 20th century eugenics movement that was expressed, chillingly, in policies in Nazi Germany. Could people be "weeded out" for reasons unrelated to their essential humanity, including racism?

On the whole, this mapping of issues focuses on negative possibilities. Current debates over stem cell research illustrate the possibility of medical breakthroughs, based on improved genetic knowledge, in dealing with Parkinson's Disease, Alzheimer's, cancers and other diseases. In attending to the better possibilities, however, Muelder's essay is a caution that we must be alert to unexamined negative consequences. −JPW

11

The word *genome* derives from *gene* and *chromosome*. A genome is a complete set of chromosomes in the germ cell of an organism. Every human cell contains from 50,000 to 100,000 genes. In 1968 James Watson published his famous book on the double helix, which made the term *DNA* a common word in genetic research. The Department of Energy and the National Institutes of Health became involved. By 1990 the U.S. Congress had allocated $3-5 billion to be spent over 15 years in the quest to map and sequence the human genome. Other countries became involved also. Those projects were coordinated by an international group, the Human Genome Organization (HUGO).

This big science project has stimulated several groups to explore the morally and socially difficult outcomes of this highly competitive research. Interfaith conferences wrestling with these emergent problems represent Judaism, Christianity (Roman Catholic, Lutheran, Reformed, Eastern Orthodox), Islam, and Hinduism.

What are the kinds of issues which all persons should be alert to as the mapping of the genome comes to completion and its findings are applied in personal and social life? In this article I can hardly do more than list some basic topics for careful scrutiny. There are many others.

What Are the Just Limits of Patenting?

Already there are numerous marketplace issues, including the ownership of genetic materials and knowledge, patents, procedures and products. For example, does patenting a process inhibit the free flow of knowledge? Is it fair to poorer countries which do not have "big science" institutes? The investment mentality in powerful nations may compromise the vulnerable peoples in the global economy and inhibit the spread of scientific methods and research.

What Rules Should Govern Genetic Testing?

This first issue, already widespread, leads to the moral problem of genetic discrimination. This covers questions of privacy of records, health insurance, life insurance and employment as human limitations are exposed. In others words, how may the new partial and holistic genome knowledge be used and by whom? When particular accurate information on a person's genetic condition has been obtained, how may the data be used? And who will be able to use it? Some differences in inherited traits are trivial, like the shape of a nose, the slant of the eyes or the type of hair, but what of diseases like Huntington's?

Prenatal Inquiries

The problems of genetic testing come to critical moments in some prenatal inquiries, in genetic counseling, and in decisions about "normal" and "abnormal" risks and possible abortions. These may involve public policy.

Genetic Engineering

Genome studies may lead logically to the field of eugenics (genetic engineering). Should the human race use genetic knowledge and technology to try to create a more ideal individual or whole population? Who should make such a determination? The outcome could be prejudicial and even worse, disastrous.

What Are the Medically Needed Interventions?

...and should they be attempted on the somatic (bodily cells) or on a whole germline?

Two closely related problems further complicate the new scientific work with genes. What is a "real" disability? What is normal? In some cases there may need to be better public education on what is an "acceptable disability" in the home or workplace. Moreover, in genetic therapy the stages in life are relevant: sperm, eggs, cells, organs, childhood, adulthood, etc. Some churches cautiously approve interventions, including germline therapies.

Patient Rights

Intersecting all the above questions is the evolving field of "patient" rights. On such issues one's theological and moral understanding of God as Creator, of human freedom, of social solidarity versus individualism play a major role. On the global scene, America may be too market oriented and individualistic.

We Must Face Cloning

Already accomplished on animals, cloning on human beings confronts us. Divisions of judgment pervade scientific, technological, political and religious communities. The time to reflect, discuss, and consider these matters globally is now, as experimentation and application surge forward. ☙

On Cloning Human Persons

This article, not dated or published, was however written after the preceding essay on the genome project (presumably also in 2001). Here, Muelder takes up the question of human cloning. While not questioning "partial cloning" for therapeutic reasons, which he did not oppose and presumably supported, he raises serious questions about the cloning of a complete human being. The heart of his ethical argument is in his eighth point. He notes, there, that a cloned human being could not in fact be identical to the person from whom the cellular material was derived. Every person, including a cloned human being, is unique. Here, Muelder's personalism forms the basis of his ethical argument. While responsibly summarizing arguments against making human cloning illegal, Muelder concludes that a ban on cloning is the responsible policy for the foreseeable future.   **– JPW**

In an earlier article I listed a number of ethical issues which arise from the human genome project, including the question of cloning a complete human being. Because of the current discussion of such cloning I shall devote this essay to some ethical aspects of the scientific, professional, and popular treatments of the topic. For example, should attempts to clone a complete human being be forbidden by law and attempts to do so indefinitely postponed? To be sure, some scientists may try to do such cloning anyway. A [cloned] lamb named Dolly that was virtually identical to a sheep born six years earlier was announced on February 23, 1997 at the age of six months. If a sheep can be cloned, why not a human being? Of persons polled on this question, 90 percent said that human cloning should be banned. President Clinton instituted a ban on federal funding related to attempts to clone human beings.

Recently the Congress has begun to consider both policies and legislation dealing with the problems involved in cloning a complete human being. Concurrently, a Canadian religious cult, the Raelians, confirmed they were attempting such cloning. Panos

Zavos, who runs a fertility clinic in Lexington, Kentucky, and Severino Antonori, an Italian, have asserted that they plan to clone a human being in two years. These efforts show that such cloning procedures are no longer simply hypothetical issues, but urgent, scientific, medical, practical and social policy issues. They have profound ethical and theological dimensions.

I shall not focus on the technical aspects of the controversy but rather lift up some practical and ethical arguments which deserve consideration by Christians. I limit myself to one technical technique which is a variation of the procedure that produced Dolly the sheep. Dolly was the world's first cloned animal. "A needle is jabbed through an egg's protective layer and used to remove the egg's nucleus, containing most of a cell's genetic material. A second needle is used to inject a whole cell under the egg's outer layer. To complete the process, an electrical current fuses the new cell to the egg. The embryo starts to divide until within days, the mass of cells grows to about 100 and is big enough to be implanted in the surrogate mother's uterus."

Some partial cloning of a therapeutic sort already takes place. These efforts are not at issue. For example, stem-cell cloning and partial organ transplants are unaffected by any ban which is placed on planned whole human cloning. I now cite a number of moral considerations.

Should we be engaged in the moral debate or should we leave it to the scientific experts? The answer must be that we all have a moral stake. Just because something is scientifically and technically feasible does not make it morally and socially right or good. This we acknowledge in the morality of everyday life. Moreover, the public has the right to know that the "scientific experts" are not of one mind and are often influenced by competing social forces.

Does the "progress" of science justify uninhibited efforts to clone human beings? Science and technology can be privately or publicly funded to go in the most varied directions. The advancement of biological enquiries into the mysteries of the human gene has many possibilities independent of cloning a whole human being. Therefore, a ban on human cloning is not inherently anti-science.It has been argued that if the cloning efforts are banned in one country they may be attempted elsewhere (Canada or Italy, for example). But such arguments do not carry much intrinsic weight, nor do they justify ignoring the inherent hazards of cloning a complete human being.

At present these hazards are many and awesome.A ban on the latter is not an argument for banning the partial cloning of a therapeutic sort which already takes place. For example, stem-cell cloning and partial organ transplants are not at issue here.Nevertheless, we can learn from the hazards encountered in efforts to clone whole animals, particularly mammals.It is simplistic to argue that, "if human beings have the right to reproduce, what right does society have to limit the means?" The community determines the legal limits of rights and freedoms on thousands of actions in order to protect the inherent dignity of the human person.

More specifically, some argue that a wealthy couple who are childless, and are willing to clone one of the parents to replace a lost child, should be free to attempt the costly effort and hazards of cloning. But cloning has to be a matter of social policy; it is ethically dubious to establish in law a practice which all cannot enjoy. Wealth is not a determiner of justice. Some argue that a cloned baby may be an effective substitute for a mourning couple's loss of an only child. However, there are three serious objections to this: Adequate mourning does not take place in this way. A clone is physically, psychologically and spiritually not the same as a lost child. The clone has a need to develop in its own autonomy and sense of identity. The intrinsic value of a human being requires that a twin, the clone, be reared for itself and not as a substitute for another.For these and many reasons attending the risks, it is morally wrong to argue: "clone now; discuss later." A ban on cloning is the responsible policy for the foreseeable future. ☙

RESTORATIVE JUSTICE

Appearing in the April 2001 edition of the Newton church paper, this essay presents a litany of problems in the U. S. criminal justice system, including the excessively long sentences—resulting in an expanding prison population, inhumane prison conditions, distortions resulting from privatization of prisons, and a failing drug policy. Most of all, Muelder criticizes the vengeful philosophy lying behind the system, contrasting it with a restorative philosophy based on the ethical perspective that all people, including offenders and victims alike, are and should be treated as persons-in-community. What we do with our prisons is a reflection of what we are as a community.

Noting with appreciation the work of the Kairos Prison Ministry and an article by Dr. Alan Geyer (who was, incidentally, a Muelder doctoral student), Muelder defines crime as "a breach of one's solidarity with the community." That perspective, which is of a piece with Muelder's whole ethical philosophy, does not ignore the evil of crime, but it does call for positive measures which alone can deal with crime effectively. Several of these are stated briefly at the article's conclusion. His final plea is that we should "distinguish between evil and the evildoer."

Muelder does not refer, in this brief essay, to his own more detailed discussion of his basic perspective on law and penal justice, which appears in his Foundations of the Responsible Society *(at pp. 90-100). There he is quite clear in applying his personalistic ethic to the subject. For example, "Love presses justice to make its form adequate to the content of love" (p. 91), "The full personalistic norm of love is the final standard for justice in both moral and legal formulations" (p. 92), and "Except within the context of supportive love, judgment and punishment are restorative neither of social order nor of the person who has made an offense" (p. 97).*

Muelder does not relate any of this to his own Methodist commitments, but it is worth noting that concern for prison-

ers and their rehabilitation was a central ethical priority with John Wesley and the early English Methodist societies —**JPW**

The recent excellent article on the Kairos Prison Ministry prompts this essay on the crisis of America's criminal justice situation. I shall draw on a recent article on "Restorative Justice" by Alan Geyer, who is senior scholar at the Churches' Center for Theology and Public Policy, Washington, D.C. Restorative justice, like the Kairos Prison Ministry, moves beyond the usual retributive justice to the redemption possibilities that should be incorporated into the whole criminal justice system. Restorative justice conceives justice comprehensively. At one time, even in Bible history, justice meant vindictiveness, "an eye for an eye," but in the "fullness of time" (*kairos*) justice came to include loving kindness toward my offending neighbor. The criminal, the outsider, is also my neighbor. Today the movement beyond vengeance and retribution is partly practiced in the *truth and reconciliation* policy in South Africa under Mandela and Tutu. It was the essence of Martin Luther King's nonviolence.

What Is Crime?

Crime is a breach of one's solidarity with the community. The breach with persons and community cannot be restored by retribution, but by acts of atonement, forgiveness, and redemption. From this perspective the so-called "criminal justice system" is not a true system of justice at all. Our system comprises not only the wardens, judges, prosecutors, lawyers, offenders, victims, and guards, but also the American culture of violence, politics, and morality of vengeance which has its apex in efforts to make capital punishment a way of justice. Justice Blackman, who wrote *Roe vs. Wade*, said in 1994, "I shall no longer tinker with the machinery of death: The death penalty has failed."

What Is Justice?

The term *justice* has become a slippery slope of meanings and practices from Plato's harmony of social classes in the Republic to unlimited revenge for personal injury and even to "let the market place decide." In this situation we need fresh thinking with real concern for persons-in-community when we define justice. Within the Bible we note a wonderful development from the idea of vengeful retaliation to the priority of concern for the poor and disinherited, thus a moral development from a negative emphasis to a positive one for restitution, atonement, uniting love with restoration. Canon Alan Geyer proposes the following: "Justice is the structure of human rights and responsibilities which best expresses God's covenant-love." This would change our criminal justice system.

What is the present situation in our prisons and jails? Three-fourths of our new inmates are African-American or Hispanic. Color-lining in arrests and sentencing is rampant. One-third of America's young African-American males are now in prison, on parole, or on probation. Furthermore, we are caught in a privatized prison-industrial complex. We have underdeveloped preventive institutions and after-care ministries. The two million persons in jail or prison are four times what it was 20 years ago. This rate of incarceration is matched only in Russia. It is five times the rate in Canada and most European countries. This rate is especially shocking because the crime rate has declined each year over the past decade. There is no clear relationship of cause and effect except of a trend in the "get tough" movement that advocates harsher sentences, mandatory minimum sentencing laws, bigger and fewer human prisons, minimal rehabilitation programs, decline in parole, militancy in the drug laws, the failing war on drugs, three-strikes-and-you're-out laws. About 3,500 Americans (disproportionately African-American) sit on death row.

Vengeful penology is aided and abetted by the recent growth of the commercial prison-industrial complex which has become a big $140 billion piece of the American economy. This privatization of imprisonment, like hotels, demands high occupancy in its institutions. Low occupancy is a drag on profits. Making prisoners into commodities encourages harsh discipline, low budgets for rehabilitation, minimal job training, poor pay scales for employees, and inmate warehousing. But the drive goes on for bigger prisons.

What Values Should Our Culture Demand?

• Nonviolent sanctuary for prisoners and separating the violent from those amenable to *restorative justice.*

• Redefining crime as essentially a violation of the state to an offense toward persons and community.

• Moving from preoccupation with the past to a focus on problem-solving and preparation for the future.

• Bringing the injurers and the victims face to face to encourage repentance, atonement, and forgiveness.

• Encouraging faith in restorative justice.

Such values are not blind to the reality of personal and social evil, but they are redemptive realism. They distinguish between evil and the evildoer. ☯

THE CHALLENGE OF TERROR

This unpublished article, bearing no date, was written soon after the traumatic attacks on the World Trade Center and the Pentagon on 9/11. Muelder was immediately critical of the response by President Bush and much of the American public for invoking the vocabulary of war and crusade. In its references to history, the essay follows the typology of Roland Bainton, who wrote of the three major Christian types of response to war as Pacifism, Crusade, and Just War (in his 1960 volume, Christian Attitudes Toward War and Peace*).*

Muelder repeats here his long-standing opposition to the rhetoric and realities of war, using the crisis of 9/11 as an illustration of what he considers to be their practical as well as ethical flaws. His drawing upon James Carroll's distinction between the language of law rather than that of violence in dealing with terrorists leads to the conclusion that "the language of justice is the language of law," while "the language of war is the language of violence, retribution, and vengeance."

This article, written prior to the U.S. invasion of Iraq in 2003, includes Muelder's prophetic insight into how in using "the language of crusades and war, one is in danger of enflaming millions of people who should not be aroused against the USA." That view was to be stunningly confirmed. **–JPW**

Two dimensions of American life exhibited themselves as symbols of solidarity following the terrorist attacks of September 11th in New York and Washington, D.C., namely religious faith and patriotism. The former expressed the solidarity of compassion and tolerance; the latter expressed the national secular unity in the display of flags. The former produced great and innumerable interfaith gatherings in churches and stadiums. The latter called forth unifying speeches by the president, governor and mayors, and the singing of "God Bless America" and "The Star Spangled Banner."

Christians, Jews, Muslims, Sikhs and many other religious bodies avowed their sense of tolerance for American pluralism. Even in political gatherings, the ultimate affirmation of spiritual unity and community showed a common "God Bless America" appeal.

In times of crises, religion and nationalism have a tendency to coalesce, and hatred for the enemy is fanned to a fever pitch, challenging the basic values of the nation.

Two major symbols of American life were attacked on 9/11. The World Trade Towers symbolized the economic power and practices of globalization. The Pentagon represented the military might of the United States. It is significant that both of these were attacked on the same day. For many people in the world, these are signs of American arrogance.

In addressing the nation the president said: "Our grief has turned to anger and anger to resolution. Whether we bring our enemies to justice or bring justice to our enemies, justice will be done." This was followed by a declaration of war against the "terrorists." It is this language of war and its practical application that needs analysis and the response of the churches.

The use of the categories of war, combined with the words of crusade, has dangerous implications about which the churches have a long tradition. This tradition is worth reviewing, and must bring the inter-faith meetings and the political-nationalist meetings noted above into dialogue with each other.

For its first three centuries, Christianity was solidly a peace community. Christians were expected not to serve in the military. The spirit of Jesus and his explicit teachings taught Christians to endure persecution, including death in the Roman arena, if necessary. In some places, Christians were not allowed to take communion if they served in the army.

Beginning with Emperor Constantine, who used Christianity to unify his empire, the notion of a "just war" was introduced and was supported by leaders like Ambrose and Augustine. Little by little and through the centuries, the Just War Theory became the dominant theory, and pacifism became a minority position, even a sectarian one, usually identified with groups like the Society of Friends and the Mennonites.

A third position arose in the Middle Ages, the Crusades. This referred to the period when Roman popes advocated military crusades to win the Holy Land from the dominant Muslims. The period lasted about two and a half centuries. The idea of a Christian Crusade has been denounced and arouses in Muslim minds a militant conflict between Christians and Islam. It is unfortunate that President Bush has used this term, for it has bad historical overtones.

It is probably a serious blunder for the president to use words like "war" in dealing with terrorism for the following reasons:

1. At the present time, as columnist James Carroll has said, it is better to use the language of law, not of violence, in dealing with terrorists. The language of justice is the language of law. The latter is the language of legal accountability. The language of war is the language of violence, retribution and vengeance.

2. War is declared against political entities. Terror is done by individuals and groups outside the boundaries of political authority. Power is a term used to express the will of a people constrained by reason and law and amenable to courts. If one uses the language of crusades and war, one is in danger of enflaming millions of people who should not be aroused against the USA.

3. War is a very imprecise term. Once war is declared, it tends to lose boundaries, and violence becomes general. Innocent groups (like the American-Japanese in World War II) may become victims. War defies legal enforcement and may itself become terror.

4. Talk of war focuses on results, not methods. The great developments of American democracy have also seen development of law and constitutional discipline. To respond to terrorism with violence may cause the terrorists to win their objectives.

5. War generates its own momentum and may cause a huge loss of human rights. In war, criticism of the government often leads to suspicion of disloyalty, or worse. Fortunately, there are many cautions by respected voices in this crisis. When the Oklahoma bombing terror occurred, some said immediately, "It must be the Arabs," only to learn eventually that it was an American.

In the twisted logic of terrorists, the believers among them feel that in their despair they have nothing to lose. Their despair may be racially, economically, politically or gender oriented. Their despair needs to be turned to hope, and hope mixed with compassion is a mission of the churches. ◈

FREEDOM AND SECURITY

This article, also appeared prior to the U. S. invasion of Iraq, but subsequent to the more broadly international invasion of Afghanistan (published in the Newton church paper in January, 2002). It was a further response to that pivotal event. Here, Muelder's stance as a principled civil libertarian was expressed, along with his decades-old commitments to the ecumenical movement. This particular essay emphasizes the 1948 ecumenical concept of the Responsible Society as the theological-ethical basis for freedom.

We are, according to that concept, "created and called to be a free being, responsible to God and (our neighbor)." Thus, anything that deprives us of the possibility of acting responsibly toward God and neighbor is "a denial of God's intention." Muelder found the basic concept to be directly relevant to the situation in Afghanistan. Quoting again from the ecumenical formula, "persons are not made for the State but the State for persons. Persons are not made for production, but production for persons." And then, "for a society to be responsible under modern conditions it is required that the people have freedom to control, to criticize and to change their governments, that power be made responsible by law and tradition, and be distributed as widely throughout the whole community."

Muelder did not, in this article, take up the utterly oppressive rule of the Taliban government in Afghanistan, with its total intolerance of any form of religion or of behavior considered to be contrary to the Taliban's strict conception of Islam. Nor did he here discuss the role of women under that rule, although his own record of support for the empowerment of women was very progressive. The article was written at a time when the Taliban movement was understood to be defeated beyond recovery; the relevant issue was how the United States and allies would work with progressive elements in Afghanistan society to create a very different kind of state. So his appeal was to approach this task positively and not punitively. **—JPW**

In response to the terrorist attacks in New York, Washington, D.C., and Pennsylvania, President Bush declared war on terrorism. He marshaled the military might of the USA to hunt for and bring to justice the person of Osama bin Laden, a "war" which is still in progress. The alleged guilty parties to terrorist acts are to be tried in ill-defined "military tribunals" and widespread security measures are being advocated. At the airports these measures are being institutionalized and implemented. When long-time guarantees of liberty for accused persons are being advocated in the trying of accused "terrorists," the response is often "trust us." To such assurances the reply by historically grounded civil liberties is that of John Adams: this is a government of laws, not of men.

In this article I wish to urge the churches to recall their own historical achievements in the field of human rights, their formulation of the "idea of the responsible society." Instead of just seeking ways to "win the war" in Afghanistan, we might better ask: "What are the foundations of a just and lasting peace?" During the crisis of the Great Depression, the World Council of Churches in process of formation, held a great conference in Oxford, England, in 1937. The findings of the Oxford conference became the basis of the ecumenical social ethics of the World Council in 1948 which met in Amsterdam. At that time the tensions between the capitalist and the communist oriented nations were just as keen as the tensions are today between the Christian and the Islamic social orders. There was a desire to formulate and develop a third force politically and economically. If we ask not how to win the present war, but what the conditions should be for justice and peace in the world, we might well begin with the idea of the "responsible society" which was formulated in 1948.

I shall concentrate on that idea in this article. It is necessary that a standard be formulated that is relevant to show human religious obligation to God and which makes contact with the best sober constructive work of secular agencies such as the Human Rights Commission of the United Nations.

Amsterdam said: "We have to learn afresh to speak boldly in Christ's name both to those in power and to the people, to oppose terror, cruelty and race discrimination, to stand by the outcast, the prisoner, and the refugee. We have to make of the church in every place a voice for those who have no voice, and a home where every man will be at home. We have to learn afresh together what is the duty of Christian man or woman in industry, in agriculture, in politics, in the professions and in the home."

This voice must learn afresh to say "no" to everyone who sows the seeds of war or who teach that war is inevitable.

Out of the ecumenical debate emerged the following definition of "the responsible society": "Man (human beings) is (are) created and called to be a free being, responsible to God and his neighbor. Any tendencies in state or society depriving man of the possibility of acting responsibly are a denial of God's intention for (human beings) and their work of salvation, a responsible society is one where freedom is the freedom of human beings who acknowledge responsibility to justice and public order, and where those who hold political authority or economic power are responsible for its exercise to God and the people whose welfare is affected by it."

When we think through the practical applications of this comprehensive axiom of responsibility and how to help Afghanistan and the new nations of Africa and Asia achieve order and stability, it is well to give concrete form to the following guidelines. These were also formulated at the World Council Assembly in 1948.

"Persons[20] must never be made a mere means for political or economic ends. Persons are not made for the State but the State for persons. Persons are not made for production, but production for persons. For a society to be responsible under modern conditions it is required that the people have freedom to control, to criticize and to change their governments, that power be made responsible by law and tradition, and be distributed as widely as possible throughout the whole community. It is required that economic justice and provision of equality of opportunity be established for all the members of society."

If instead of thinking so much in terms of military tribunals,

---

20. In this informally published essay, Muelder has substituted the word 'persons' for 'man' in the original 1948 World Council of Churches passage. This is further evidence that by his 90s Muelder had abandoned the male generic language characteristic of theological writings decades earlier.

we think in terms of the above standards of mutual responsibility, we can have faith in the established procedures of protecting the freedoms of persons. Having faith in other persons is one of the best foundations of security in society. In the past weeks we have lost too much of the faith which Christianity has tried to instill in the democratic fabric of society. ☙

MAKING A PEACE IN AFGHANISTAN

A month after writing the preceding essay, with publication in the February 2002 edition of the Newton church paper, Muelder again addressed the situation in Afghanistan. The concern now was how to assure lasting foundations for a new, democratic Afghanistan. In this writing, Muelder applauds the stance taken by the country's new President Karzai, as summarized by the main points in the latter's opening address. Muelder pleads, then, for U. S. policies encouraging and supporting positive communication with the 56 nations of the Muslim world. The warlike rhetoric of the U. S. administration seems directly contrary to that objective, for the U.S. "Has not yet faced the question squarely: 'Why do terrorists hate the USA?' Referring to Immanuel Kant's classical essay on "Eternal Peace," Muelder asks whether the United States has observed the very first principle of not framing a peace in such a way that future wars become more likely.

It is doubtful whether Muelder became acquainted before his own death with Joseph Nye's emphasis on the distinction between "hard power" and "soft power." The former, includes military and economic power; the latter is comprised by the less direct, but no less real, capacity to influence the behavior of others—a point that was already anticipated by Franz Neumann's distinction between "control of nature" and "control of man."

*The latter, according to Neumann, always comes down to the capacity to influence others, and that is the principal point about political power. Neumann's work (*The Democratic and the Authoritarian State*) was published in 1957 and was more likely known by Muelder. In any event, the present essay clearly expresses greater confidence in "soft power" than the "hard power" upon which the Bush administration seemed primarily to rely. The essay was, of course, also written more than a year prior to the U. S. invasion of Iraq that ultimately led to protracted chaos in that country. He argues, with some* *prophetic insight, that violence should not "be carried forward by attacks on Iran, Iraq or other nations like North Korea."*

This essay, on the whole, also reflects Muelder's underlying pacifism, including its call "for the churches once more to demythologize violence and war," and that "we must see that the struggle against terrorism must be carried on with faith in democratic institutions and law enforcement." Still, it is interesting that in this essay he states as a "main point" here that "we should reaffirm as policy that war is a last resort and not the first resort." This is interesting because the traditional pacifist tradition excludes war even as a last resort!   **–JPW**

When one has not declared a formal war against another state, it may be harder to make a peace than otherwise. Making war against terrorism is like making war against poverty. The USA through military bombing, marine action and air strikes has shown its power, but it has not thus far disposed of the leaders of terror or established the secure foundations of peace in Afghanistan or among its neighbors. It has not yet faced the question squarely: "Why do terrorists hate the USA?" For that matter, the nation has not profoundly asked the question: "Why do some nations or special groups within nations hate us sufficiently to act violently against us? Do we know how to make a just and permanent peace?"

At the end of the 18th century the German philosopher, Immanuel Kant, wrote a famous essay called, "Eternal Peace." He was meaning something different from the eternal peace of a graveyard. His first principle was that nations should not put into a peace treaty any items which would be the occasion or guarantee of another war. James Carroll recently reminded us of the words of Thomas C. Schelling: "The last word might be more important that the first strike." A few historical illustrations might guide us here. World War I ended with an enemy-punishing treaty that guaranteed a future war. Hitler was a product of the Versailles Treaty. Then, World War II ended with the Allies unleashing savage air attacks against cities, especially Hiroshima and Nagasaki. In other words, the USA and the Allies lost the moral edge and initiated the era of nuclear terror. In the case of the Persian Gulf War there was a humane ending, but the sanctions which really punished the Iraqi civilian population shows that the USA has not learned how to terminate such a war. The issue is a real challenge: We can bomb powerfully, but we are challenged to show that we know how to deal with the 56 nations in the Islamic world. Each of these states has its distinctive history and character and should be respected as such. With the end of World War II, the United Nations Organization was brought into being. It should be respected and developed with the full support politically and financially by the USA.

The new government of Afghanistan as represented by Karzai is moving in the right direction. In his opening address, he emphasized some important points for constructive nation building.

1. The government will respect the religious rules of Islam in the country but rejects the negative rigidities of the Taliban. (In this respect, like all countries, there needs to be both recognition of religious heritage and separation of religious establishment and the state.) The government will protect the territorial integrity and sovereignty of Afghanistan and combat terrorism. The state respects freedom of speech and belief. Laws and internal regulations must be obeyed. Such obedience will bring peace and security.

2. There shall be respect for women, who constitute half the population. They are protected by law. The main duties of the government are security and peace. "All government posts should be given to professional people on the basis of merit." Karzai asked that his fellow Afghans outside the country would aid in the reconstruction of the country. Special attention should be given to the integrity of the use of public finances. Afghanistan needs a national army for the security of the country. The national government has a duty to reconstruct the entire educational system, using professionals from the elementary schools to the universities and academies. "Afghanistan is a member of the international community and respects all UN resolutions. We thank the United Nations for providing security and helping the reconstruction of Afghanistan." As a member of the international community Afghanistan respects all countries, especially its neighbors, and this government wants to have good relations with all neighbors on

the basis of mutual respect.

Since the USA has such a deep military involvement in the present "war," it should encourage surrender of all Al Qaeda fighters, including Bin Laden, by affirming that they will be treated according to international law. We should insist that they will not be treated by tribal law or vengeance by the Northern Alliance. Even against Bin Laden and his cohorts, they should be tried by public law. We should abandon the "dead or alive" type of rhetoric and avoid nihilist standards as used by the terrorists themselves.

We should promptly insist on using the United Nations as the instrument for handling refugees and prisoners of war. The same applies to Taliban leaders. The main point here is that we should reaffirm as policy that war is a last resort and not the first resort. This entails that violence will not be carried forward by attacks on Iran, Iraq or other nations like North Korea. It is time for the churches once more to demythologize violence and war. We must see that the struggle against terrorism must be carried on with faith in democratic institutions and law enforcement.

In these days when we sing so repeatedly, "God Bless America," we should be reaffirming our faith in the numerous small processes that make up our democratic way of life. There are many voluntary organizations that mediate personal and social life between the family and formal government. These need nurturance because they are the cell structure of participation by women and men and the training ground in democratic procedures. These cannot be superimposed from one culture to another and hence, those that are indigenous in America may not naturally make up the life-style of a predominantly Islamic society. Moreover, like the professional and neighborhood associations of America, they evolve over time from grass root levels of life, in race relations, in expressions of women's rights, and in public education showing that political structures and popular reforms grow at uneven rates. The same applies in Afghanistan.

All of the above take place today in an era of globalization. For America, this seems to mean freedom for multinational corporations to function anywhere in the world. For Afghanistan, this is obviously not its immediate agenda. ⁖

THE LADDER AND THE HOURGLASS

This essay, written in 2000, deals with an issue that was to become one of the most divisive American political conflicts four years later. Of course, U. S. policies on immigration have been debated throughout most of the nation's history, and those policies have, on the whole, resulted in this becoming (in the memorable phrase) a "nation of immigrants." Two realities have intensified the national debate since Muelder wrote this piece:

First was the climate of fear of terrorism generated by the 9/11 attacks, with widespread feelings that foreigners who might be terrorists should be prevented from entering the country as the 9/11 airplane hijackers had done.

Second is the numbers of Latin Americans crossing the border from Mexico, a factual situation generating increased xenophobia especially in southwestern states. Political conflict developed around the question whether undocumented immigrants should be given amnesty or some other method of receiving legal immigrant status. Two political realities could be noted: One was a conflict between President Bush and many, perhaps a majority within his own party, over the possibility of some kind of amnesty. The other was an evident political miscalculation by Republicans who, by their anti-immigrant rhetoric, managed to alienate large numbers of voting citizens of Latin American background.

Muelder's appeal here is to the church. Unspoken is his universalistic ethical perspective, in terms of which even national borders should not be taken too seriously. If God is God of all, and if we are to regard everybody on earth as our neighbors, then national borders are barriers, inhibiting our being the human family God has intended. Muelder doesn't make that point here, and it is possible he would have considered some degree of cultural unity within a nation to have at least relative value—with resultant implications for immigration policy. But, given that "mankind is the unit of cooperation," there are

deeper implications to be drawn from Muelder's overall eco-
nomic perspective. Could one not argue that there will always
be problems with immigration as long as there are huge dis-
parities of wealth and income among the world's countries?
Population flow across the U.S.-Canadian border has not been
much of a problem on either side, not even in respect to Que-
bec where there are substantial linguistic differences, for the
standard of living between these two countries is close enough
to being equal that there is not a huge economic incentive for
people to migrate. Would that not also be the case to the south if
the economic levels of Mexico and Central American countries
were much closer to those in the United States?

It may go without saying that modern means of commu-
nication and transportation render national boundaries all the
more porous.

Another aspect of Muelder's essay is worth noting: that
is the positive value of waves of immigration to the United
States. He remarks that some of the immigrants are highly
trained professionals. Of course, a side effect of that reality is
that this "brain-drain" further impoverishes poorer countries,
making it even less likely that they would be able to approach
the American standard of living.   **–JPW**

The church in America has been challenged by the changing
pattern of immigration. Each wave, whether prompted by en-
slavement, thirst for religious freedom, economic need, or by political aspiration has fed the idea of some kind of assimilation of
the immigrants. What was called the "new immigration" of 1900
has marked differences from that which may be peaking (or is it?)
in 2000.

I shall contrast these modes of immigration and their chal-
lenges to assimilation by two figures of speech, the ladder and the
hourglass, to borrow metaphors from M. Suarez-Orosco, who is
co-director of the Harvard Immigration project. Let us begin with
some statistics. During the first decade of the 20th century about
8,800,000 immigrants arrived. By 1998, the United States had
over 25 million immigrants. Up to 1950, nearly 90 percent of all

immigrants were Europeans or Canadians; today over 50 percent of all immigrants are from Latin America and 27 percent are from Asia. By region of origin, in 1997, 17 percent were Europeans, 27 percent were Asians, and 51 percent were Latin Americans.

Large scale immigrations of unfamiliar persons feeds fear of foreigners, called xenophobia. It has major implications of two kinds, economic and socio-cultural. Debates today are rekindled over "people of color" and over bi-lingual and multi-cultural education and assimilation. Many people like to think of the past course of integration of foreigners as climbing the ladder of progress: (a) the first generation makes a "clean break" with their past from one country and political-economic condition to a new start; (b) then comes a process of homogenization into a predominantly white, Protestant, and middle-class orientation; and (c) finally there is the assumption of arrival at the "good life" which becomes progressively better in the third and fourth generations. The reality has been, of course, quite different. "Utopia" has been for the few.

The reality for today is closer to the figure of an hourglass than of a ladder. In the hourglass, the favored classes are above and the masses of new immigrants are below, and many persons are trickling down from the top. The climb up the hourglass is exceedingly difficult, as the plight of the urban under-classes shows.

Immigration today has many surprises. The well-educated and skilled may arrive at the top, joining the knowledge-intensive industries. Indeed, immigrants are over-represented in the category of people with doctorates. In 1998, half of all "entering physics graduate students were foreign-born." Thirty-two percent of all scientists and engineers working in California's famed Silicon Valley are immigrants. A third of all Nobel Prize winners in the USA have been immigrants. Indeed, in 1999 all (100 percent) of U.S. Nobel Prize winners were immigrants. They tend to settle in safe middle-class suburban areas. Many immigrants have needed no ladder to climb.

However, most recent immigrants have entered America in the lower part of the hourglass and have not climbed up very far. Many youths trickle farther down. Today's global economy is unforgiving of immigrants with few skills and credentials. Youth of color from poorly educated backgrounds fall into this group. Their optimism and hope is snuffed out by intense segregation, inferior schools, violent neighborhoods, and structural and interpersonal racism.

The historic contrast between the era of the ladder-up and the trap of the hourglass constitutes a major challenge to the educational and spiritual resources of both church and state. The old assumptions of generational assimilation no longer hold. Conflict and dissent in urban America require creative efforts in public and private reconciliation. Will the churches inspire the nation to rise to the challenge or go their own segregated way? ☜

THE FACE OF HUNGER IN AMERICA

In this article, written for the Newton church paper, Mu-elder focused briefly on his life-long concern for economic justice. The occasion, at the end of 1999, was a National Council of Churches policy priority on dealing with poverty in America. As in all such writings, statistics need constant up-dating. In this case, the discouraging fact is that in the half-decade since this was written there had been so little change, and what change there was represented a small increase in the number of people living in poverty.

For instance, Muelder (using figures presented by Kay Bengston of the Lutheran Office for Public Affairs) wrote of 34.5 million Americans below the poverty line in 1998, which represented 12.7 percent of the population. Official figures for 2005 showed 38.2 million, or 13.3%. 1998 was at the peak of an economic boom, 2005 was a year or so into an economic re-covery following the downturn that began around 2001. Still, the figures show the numbers of poor people to be stable and, if anything, getting a bit worse.

Muelder's article is too brief to offer much in the way of solutions to this on-going problem. He does emphasize increases in the minimum wage and better access to food stamps. But, as a response to the NCC call, he urges the churches to be strong advocates for the poor—thus echoing again the call of the 1948 World Council message that the church must be "a voice for those who have no voice."   **–JPW**

As the church moves from the festival of Thanksgiving into the season of Advent, many appeals by great causes come to our attention. The National Council of Churches, of which The United Methodist Church is a member, is urging its member denominations to adopt certain policy priorities for 2000-2001. Among these is "the face of hunger in America." This article focuses on this hunger crisis for our discussion.

Kay Bengston of the Lutheran Office for Public Affairs brings the situation to our urgent attention. The prospering American economy is not reaching everyone. According to the U.S. Census, while family income between 1979 and 1999 rose by 30 percent for the top fifth of families, the bottom fifth of families saw their incomes fall by six percent. Some feel powerless in a complex economy over which they have little or no control. They struggle desperately to survive.

Hunger in America is real. It is a condition of poverty. In 1998, 34.5 million Americans (12.7 percent of the population) lived in poverty. 18.9 percent of all American children under age 18 were poor. This rate is higher than it was 30 years ago and is higher than in most industrialized nations. In families with a female householder and no husband present, the poverty rate where children were under age six, was 54.8 percent. This rate was more than five times the rate for children under six in married couple families, where it was 10.1 percent. Kay Bengston points out that since 1995 the number of poor children has reached the highest level recorded since data on this matter were first collected in 1979.

The real hunger-poverty situation is obscured by the fact that while 17 million people participate in the Food Stamp program, this is a dramatic decrease of 27 percent in the last four years. The actual situation is that though poverty among children dropped by three percent in 1997, the number of children receiving food stamps dropped by 10 percent.

Why was there a decline in food stamp use in the midst of a vibrant economy? There are two main reasons: (1) uneven implementation of welfare reform, such as not informing people that they qualified for food stamps, and (2) eliminating the eligibility of most legal immigrants. As a result, from November 1, 1998 to October 31, 1999, the U.S. Conference of Mayors report that they received requests for emergency food assistance in 85 percent of the cases investigated.

Hunger is a consequence of poverty. The poor tend to be powerless. They need advocates; and the church should be a strong advocate. Both private and public sectors of society must be aroused. Wages must be increased for some and other support may require subsidies.

One avenue of assistance is passing the Hunger Relief Act sponsored by Senator Edward Kennedy (D-MA) and Arlen Spector (R-PA). This Act restores food stamp benefits to legal immigrants based on need. It also proves that families with high shelter costs may receive greater food stamp allotments.

We need also to increase the minimum wage and provide better access to job training to raise skill levels and earning capabilities. ☙

REFLECTIONS ON THEOLOGY
AND PHILOSOPHY

On June 1, 2004, less than a month before his death, Walter Muelder gave an extraordinary interview in a program documenting the history of the Boston University School of Theology. This reflection, from the interview conducted by Marilyn Costanzo, deals with some of the most profound issues in theology and philosophy. Aside from the sheer lucidity of this 97-year-old's mind, Muelder's remarks illustrate his continuing identification with the personalist tradition. At the same time, he expresses his views with great humility. At the end of a very long life, he is impressed by how little we can know for sure!

What can he mean by saying, "theologically speaking, I'm very agnostic"? In this context, that is not the same thing as lacking faith; rather, he seems to mean what he declared earlier: "faith is not the same as knowing." Still, he is willing to place a question mark behind all of the great questions. What is one to make of this? One finds here yet another example of Muelder's consummate honesty.

Perhaps, echoing a comment by Paul Tillich, there is a kind of intellectual justification by faith. To be willing to confront one's uncertainties honestly is to exhibit a concern for truth and a confidence in an ultimate reality that sustains truth. His observation that "philosophy is more ultimate than theology" will be rejected by many theologians, but that is perhaps his way of saying that no theology is worthy of consideration that is unwilling to face the truth question. Do the symbols and myths and stories and metaphors of theology pertain to reality? Are they amenable to testing? As a personalist, Muelder can pose that question by asking, are they coherent in respect to all we can know?

One notes here his continuing openness to truth as it may be conveyed in religious traditions other than Christian—a quality of openness the world desperately needs in these years after Muelder's passing. At the same time, he understands that one cannot remain aloof. So he concludes, "I belong to Jesus. You have to belong somewhere." We are thus reminded of his lifelong commitment to the love ethic as exemplified by Jesus. About its ultimate significance, he seems to say, we must remain intellectually humble. But it continues to be a foundation upon which we can stand.   **–JPW**

Theology raises questions that you can only tackle in philosophy. In other words, as a discipline, philosophy is more ultimate than theology. That made me become a philosophical theologian. One of my heroes was Harry Emerson Fosdick. I discovered him in college. He satisfied me. But those liberal theologians—in fact, all liberal theologians that I know—are willing to put a question mark behind such questions as "Is there life after death?", "What is the nature of ultimate reality?" and so forth. They admit they don't *know,* and faith is not the same as *knowing.* Knowing has an element of faith. So these issues are interplaying all the time.

What I appreciated as a student at Boston was that, whether it was Brightman or Knudson or somebody else at the CLA (Boston University College of Liberal Arts), or whoever I was studying with, they kept the dialogue open between theologians and philosophers. I remember when I was reading (Henry Nelson) Wieman, "What is the difference between philosophy and religion?" Philsophy talks about vitamins and minerals. Theology talkes about spinach, carrots, lettuce, potatoes. It takes a concrete risk. The other is still dealing with fundamental elements.

Theologically speaking, I'm very agnostic. Philosophically speaking, I am willing to risk, still risk, the Personalist hypothesis. But I know it's a hypothesis. Since religion is a questing, a searching, a seeking, and so forth, you risk something. But as a modern person what you risk saying you know is not *the* absolute truth and that nobody else has it either. You have faith in that. As I studied philosophical theologians, whether they were Fosdick, Hawking, Tillich or whatever, the exploration outruns the answer. That's where I am. Still.

So, I can't say as Strickland or Marlatt would have, "Well, on certain days I'm a Buddhist, on certain days I'm a Hindu," and so forth and so on. We had a swami, and I didn't find him dogmatic about what he was saying. When he went to India for six weeks, he asked me if I would take over his services. I had no trouble doing that. I belong to the Christian tradition. And, as I said in my last chapel speech to the entering class of '93, "I belong to Jesus. You have to belong somewhere." ᢒᢧ

WALTER MUELDER'S LAST SPEECH

Muelder had been invited to address the retired clergy of the New England Conference of The United Methodist Church in June, 2004. He chose to challenge his fellow retirees to remain active in the church and, above all, to keep calling it back to its basic nature. At the church's 2004 General Conference, concluded a few weeks earlier, efforts had been made to change some of the liberal theological positions that Muelder held dear. In particular, there had been attempts to diminish or abandon the "quadrilateral." This four-fold understanding of the sources for theological reflection has, for more than a generation, helped guide United Methodists in their use of Scripture, tradition, reason and experience. No one of these, alone, has been considered adequate as a basis for the theological task—indeed, no two or three of them alone.

At the 1988 General Conference, when revisions in references to the "quadrilateral" were last undertaken, the primacy of Scripture was emphasized. But Scripture alone was not understood to be sufficient without reference to centuries of church tradition, reasoned scriptural interpretation, and contemporary individual and corporate experience of Christians. The "quadrilateral," in fact, could be seen as not unlike the "emergent coherence" forming the heart of Muelder's ethical method. So he writes, "this four-fold coherence is essential for maintaining authoritative doctrine and practice."

His final sentence is a direct appeal to retired clergy to use their contacts. Their ministry must continue throughout their span of life, even in retirement. While no longer engaged in pastoral ministry, they could still influence events in a positive way. By saying that "we are a part of (the contemporary church's) ongoing dialogue..." Walter George Muelder was, in his own person, making a larger point: If a 97-year-old man could remain so vitally in connection with the church and participate so fully in influencing other persons and events, what excuse would anybody else have for neglecting those responsibilities?

Within three days, he would be gone, leaving this challenge to his listeners that as long as life continues we still have our work to do. **—JPW**

We retired ministers have an ongoing role to play in the conflicts, such as those on homosexuality, which threatened to split the church at the last General Conference.

We are in constant dialogue with clergy and laity who are rightfully troubled by these issues. We can help hold the church together by reminding people to think comprehensively and holistically about these questions. The positions taken by militant opponents are often narrowly based by appeals to the authority of single verses of Scripture as decisively conclusive.

We need to remind the whole church that Methodism has a four-fold basis for making authoritative positions, namely: Scripture, tradition, reason and experience. It is the coherence of these explorations that is authoritative. No literal appeal to isolated Scripture passages is sufficient. We have to understand the historical nature of Scripture as a whole and relate any passage of the Bible as a whole to the evolving tradition—both within the biblical period, to historical Methodism, to the best scientific reasoning, and to a comprehensive awareness of evolving experience. This four-fold coherence is essential for maintaining authoritative doctrine and practice.

As retired ministers, we are constantly in contact with members of the contemporary church and hence, we are part of its ongoing dialogue to maintain the unity of the church. ☙

Part II

Selected Writings

*The Muelder archive at Boston University School of Theology con-
tains some 360 of Muelder's published articles and reviews, in addition to 300 previously unpublished lectures, speeches and sermons. These
writings span 70 years of productive intellectual leadership. Five of the
previously unpublished works have been selected for inclusion here, further illustrating the breadth of Muelder's interests and contributions.*

SPOT VALUES AND FIELD VALUES

*This brief essay was a Boston University baccalaureate
sermon, dated May 18, 1997, when Muelder was already 90
years old. Borrowing a distinction from half a century earlier by
Harvard philosopher William Ernest Hocking, Muelder illustrates and elaborates its ethical applicability. The sermon-essay
argues that particular events, causes, successes or failures are ultimately meaningless unless they are contained within a broader fabric of moral conviction. The distinction can be related to
similar moral distinctions between instrumental and intrinsic
values and between penultimate and ultimate ends. In his illustrations here, Muelder, with prophetic insight, criticizes ma-
terialism as a disconnected "spot value" and questions whether
secularism can finally be fulfilling. His special application of the
distinction to the university context is both a reflection of his
own special vocation as a professor and academic administrator
and a relevant word to graduating students. His applications
of the theme of spot values and field values also illustrate his
continued life-long concern for economic justice.* **–JPW**

We are gathered here in a celebratory situation: graduates,
family, friends, and faculty to congratulate each other and
to praise God for graciously bringing us to a day of arrival and
commencement. We thank God for the graduates. We are here to
acknowledge Ultimate Good, which is the ground for our transition from one stage of life to the next. A datable goal has been
achieved. Let us call it a *spot value*. It makes us feel good because it
conforms to and is confirmed by the rules of academia, that is, the

field values of the courses and of the schools and colleges.

I would like to have us consider *spot values* and *field values* in the setting of ethics and religion. Every day we are experiencing spot values in the context of field values.

About 50 years ago Prof. William Ernest Hocking used this felicitous distinction when we were discussing the Iron Curtain, National Socialism, McCarthyism, the Soviet Union and their relation to truth and justice. A spot value is any concrete or datable experience which is valued, such as this morning's breakfast, this Commencement Day, yesterday's baseball game, a job offer, a labor-management negotiation, a bill passed by the legislature, a judgment in the courts, a concert, or a scientific discovery. A field value is the set of rules or standards which controls the spot value and gives it positive meaning. It is the normative context.

For example, in a sports event like a baseball game only one team can win, but the losing team can nevertheless go forward if it feels that the game was played according to the rules and if the norms of sportsmanship were upheld. But if the losing team feels strongly that these field values were violated, then the team cannot gracefully accept defeat. *So the general observation is that the field values must be in order if the spot values are to be in order.* Sometimes games are played to be won at any price. Success is the only thing, some say. When such a violation of field values occurs, there may be a breakdown in the future relations of the teams and of the schools they represent. The latter may be disbarred by the athletic association, players may be suspended and fined. Spot values are scarce values in that they are datable. Success is a scarce value, but people can tolerate loss if they believe that the field values are still intact. A community is held together by its field values. One thing is characteristic of field values like fair play and justice: both sides in a contest can win, for the more the field values are observed the more they increase.

Permit me one more illustration. In a labor-management dispute the spot value is the contract. The contract as negotiated may not be what either side wholly aimed for. But, if both sides feel that the bargaining was done in "good faith" and that power on either side was not used unfairly, the contending parties can live with the results. Since the relevant field values are in order, the parties will have future opportunities to negotiate. But when the field values of collective bargaining are violated, serious trouble may lie ahead. American labor history is replete with both peaceful settlements and with turmoil.

All life is a problem of spot values in relation to field values. Means and ends must be coherent if life is to be harmonious. People whose attention is primarily focused on the datable spot values, having failed to cultivate the relevant field values, are destined to have negative outcomes whether in their jobs, families, recreation and so on. We are by nature communitarian beings with spiritual aspirations and needs. Some, however, are so secularized that their existence seems to be but an aggregate of fleeting experiences.

Some modern interpreters rejoice in the secularization of one sphere of life after another, what they call the emancipation from the mental tyranny of church, synagogue and religions generally. And there is much evidence that our secular culture is drifting into an obsession with spot values to the neglect of spirituality, justice, proportion and wisdom. The English historian, Norman Davies, observes that economic pretensions have "moved into the void left by the decline of religion and of moral consensus and are seen as the main preoccupation of public policy, a panacea for social ills and the source even of private contentment." (*Europe*, p. 605)

I do not make a simple equation of the decline of popular participation in church and synagogue life with an eclipse of field values, but Jesus was not wrong when he observed that people do not achieve eternal life by collecting abundance, or by prodigality, or by ignoring the poor, the sick and the imprisoned. In Jesus we see the perfect integration of spot values and field values. Jesus was not a first-century fundamentalist. Life is not a legalistic performance even by religious rules. It is still the case that we need to love God with all our hearts, souls, mind and strength and our neighbors as ourselves. There is a moral order that we *find* in reality and do *not make* according to our own immediate desires. There is a social order to which we are accountable and for which we are responsible. There is a "We" from which we cannot escape.

One of the measures of our individualistic secularity is the widening gap between rich and poor and the tendency to regard the poor as the "undeserving poor." Whether we note the incomes of the CEOs in certain profit-seeking corporations; or the salaries of basketball, football, or baseball stars; or the incomes of certain entertainers and broadcasters; or even the salaries of some in the professions, we cannot help being impressed by secular concentration on the "bottom line" and the corresponding drift of talent. Are true field values controlling these spot values? Perhaps great sportsmanship, team solidarity, and the sports themselves are deteriorating? Should we in the educated classes be speaking up more in protest? My field values tell me that there is something gross and even obscene when basketball coaches have contracts for $70 million.

In conscience I should also lift up as illustrative the relation of spot values to field values in the field of health-care delivery. Health is concretely individual, but it is also a social concern. From the days of Cain and Abel we are admonished to be our brother's keeper. But what is the drift in the controlling field value of health care delivery? The commercialization of health care in the HMOs and "for profit" corporations in "assisted living" facilities challenge both professional and general social ethics. The notion that the market is the just arbiter of who gets what and how much health care contradicts the historical field values of medicine as a profession and the Judeo-Christian heritage with respect to the care of the sick and the dying. Health insurance is a noble idea, but is it right that for-profit insurance companies should determine how babies come into the world and how long new mothers should be hospitalized?

Can universities and colleges assist in establishing the principles or norms for managing the spot values of contemporary society? Has the secularization of higher education in the last 50 years contributed to the problem or to the solution? Once, liberal arts contributed to both an intellectual and a social consensus, but is education now caught in the drift of fragmentation? Are the disciplines inward looking or community oriented?

The answer to these questions is not unequivocal. In one sense the answer is "yes," that the university can help. Each discipline or course has its *ecology* embedded in the ecology of the School where it is offered. The answer is less clear about the ecology of the college in the University, except administratively. There is no guarantee that a student pursuing, for example, the spot value of administering an elder care facility has been nurtured in the ecology of the urban poor.

A great transformation has taken place in higher education in the past 50 years. It is bigger, more diverse, more research oriented, more democratic and global. Along with democratization there has been an explosion of specialization and even of fragmentation. Some concern for transdisciplinary understanding has occurred, but comparatively little interdisciplinary activity takes place. Yet life outside the university of today is not ordered in the same way as the curriculum. Agencies of the community do not correspond to majors in college departments. Graduates soon learn that they need on-the-job training. On both sides there is much in-house introversion. These developments are, to a degree, inevitable. Human beings are finite and divide their work into small manageable units of labor. Yet, a student and a citizen often lack a sense of the whole and of what rules apply to what concentrations of activity. Only the insiders understand the jargon.

The problems of spot and field values in the universities are beset by yet other in-house factors of misunderstanding. (1) The winds of doctrine blow with more storms of criticism than with the breezes of constructive creation. (2) The tides of method line the shores of scholarship with the debris of destructive analysis. (3) Special analysis features the *relativism* of everything, or it *historicizes* everything, or *genderizes* everything, or does special pleading for *racial and ethnic groups*. As a result, nothing has objective or universal significance. The spot values of history, gender, race or ethnicity absorb field values into themselves by special pleading. Some popular movements even try to show that all language is but the manifestation of power, not of reality or truth. Criticism is king. Scientific discovery has its eye on the patent office.

But these things need not be. Meaning rises from the particular to the whole; it descends from the whole to the part. Boston University has an inclusive ecology in that its charter is inclusive and bars discrimination based on gender, race, class or religion.

Its inclusiveness has goals such as virtue, learning and piety. On the frieze of this chapel are the shields for all areas of enquiry. Their location on the chapel means that the ecology of the whole is transfigured in true worship.

A person is invited to graduate with a magnificent spiritual and moral as well as technically competent set of field values. The ecology of the university's traditional passion still lives. I will illustrate this persuasion of mine as I conclude these remarks by citing Martin Luther King, Jr.'s testimony. As you crossed the plaza you passed the statue of King, the Nobel Prize winning leader of the civil rights movement, which was a series of spot value events sustained by the field values of nonviolent social action. In his autobiography, *Stride Toward Freedom*, he related this body of field values to his education at Boston University.

"The next steps of my intellectual pilgrimage to nonviolence came during my doctoral studies at Boston University. Here I had the opportunity to talk to many exponents of nonviolence, both students and visitors to the campus...I studied philosophy at Boston University under Edgar S. Brightman and L. Harold DeWolf...[21] (Personal Idealism is the theory) that the clue to the meaning of ultimate reality is found in personality...It gave me metaphysical and philosophical grounding for the idea of a personal God, and it gave me a metaphysical basis for the dignity and worth of all human personality."

In King's career there were failures and successes, victories and defeats, but always the field values to redeem, to heal, to strive for global justice.

Dear friends, neither you nor I is Martin Luther King, Jr., but the message should be clear. Whether you play baseball, or negotiate a labor-management contract, whether you perform in the arts or do health care research and delivery, whether you are a scientist, a teacher, or a lawyer, the spot values of your experience require a coherent body of field values. If these have been developed well while at Boston University, you are indeed blessed. ☙

---

21. King had included Dr. Muelder in this list of formative influences on his thinking, a point that Muelder, with characteristic modesty, neglects to mention!

THE MERITS OF AFFIRMATIVE ACTION

One of the tragic legacies of the centuries of slavery and racial discrimination in American society—and of the subordinate status of women from time immemorial—has been lack of opportunity for previously marginalized people. Even with the removal of legal and institutional barriers, such people continued to be disadvantaged. The restoration of legal equality of opportunity—imperfect as that itself has been—did not confer factual equality. Accordingly, a logical next step after achievement of the major legal goals of desegregation during the 1960s was for American society to address this lagging inequality of opportunity.

It was as though the previously disadvantaged, while formally equal in the races of life, had to start several yards behind the previously—and still—advantaged. The concept of "affirmative action" took hold during the 1970s as a means of giving special consideration to the previously disadvantaged in selection for jobs, positions of leadership and admission to educational programs. A national debate ensued over this, with slogans about "reverse discrimination" and "discriminatory quotas" voiced to resist any special consideration. The debate continued through the 1970s, 80s, and into the 90s—with echoes still to be felt in the 21st century. The following short presentation on the subject was made to the Massachusetts Council of Churches on April 18, 1996, by a Walter Muelder who was only a year short of age 90. **–JPW**

In a general sense, Affirmative Action has a noble tradition to assist and empower disadvantaged groups (immigrants, children, the underprivileged, women, Blacks, young workers) to participate more equally in society with those not so disadvantaged. Examples are the public school system (K – 12), the state university, the GI Bill of Rights, certain scholarships, rules of admission, evaluation, promotion, tenure, appointment, and job status in both the private and public spheres of the nation. More specifically, Affirmative Action policies and programs involve compensatory, protective and preferential treatment for racial and ethnic minorities, for women, and for persons with handicapping conditions in educational and employment settings. They rest on a communitarian ethic that regards both prior historical injustice to groups of people and goals of fair democratic participation for all in both private and public life. These historic injustices and the goals of equal opportunity involve institutions which are under the control of churches, non-governmental agencies, and the state. In short Affirmative Action is goal oriented, envisaging a barrierless society which enhances personal realization and mutual responsibility. Affirmative Action is both a democratic tradition and a present need.

The theological foundations for Affirmative Action are as broad and deep as the Covenant idea in the Hebrew Scripture and the Kingdom of God ethic taught by Jesus. Salvation rests on an ethic of righteousness and grace. The ideal of the Year of Jubilee engages the Torah, the prophets and the ministry of Jesus. Human solidarity and compassion for the oppressed underlie the church's communitarian mission. Affirmative Action, resting on God's righteous rule and God's love for each person, requires the church to institute fair practices in its own life and to infuse the whole community with a spirit of rectification of past abuses and an eagerness to make possible equal opportunity for all in life and work. Indeed, the church should be a pro-active model for the whole secular order. Since law floats on a sea of ethics, the church must undergird the laws of Affirmative Action.

Affirmative Action programs may become problematic at the juncture of competing claims of competence, merit, methods of personnel selection, prior condition of advantage or disadvantage, goals of the institution, and the inclusive goals of establishing a just, participatory and sustainable society. An ahistorical individualistic, competitive, status-quo policy of alleged excellence and merit utterly misses the point of the above-stated social ethic. We are persons-in-community. Obviously, for the present, preferential selection needs to be given to some now in order that non-preferential opportunity may be the operative norm in the future.

The social reality is, for example, that many minority groups are not now fully qualified in the same representative numbers for scarce positions as the dominant group (in race or gender) in fields of education, forms of business employment, or the political arena. Those who are selected often carry a special burden because of a non-supportive job environment. As Affirmative Action changes the job scene, standards of selection will also change, reflecting the participation of those previously excluded.

It follows from all the above that Affirmative Action must be applied at the roots of society in order for the fruits of non-discrimination to be harvested. This requires an extended period of time. It means that all levels of society must be infused with programs that correct past injustices and protect those making the transition from oppression and discouragement to mutual emulation. The enemies of policies and programs are not only race and gender prejudice and oppression, but the ahistorical application of the ideas of "reverse discrimination" and "equal protection under the law." For a pool of higher qualified candidates for today's workforce and for leading scarce positions to be available, a body of such candidates must be nurtured and inspired. Much Affirmative Action is required to overcome the alienation, criminalization and incarceration of a body of youth of whom many more are now in prison than in higher education. Affirmative Action must be designed to overcome the alienation. ☙

ETHICAL ISSUES IN BUSINESS

This address was presented to the Clergy-Industry Relations Department of the National Association of Manufacturers" on May 7, 1963. It includes a number of themes drawn from Muelder's life-long interest in issues of economic ethics. But it is noteworthy in another important respect: Muelder was directly challenging a powerful national organization based largely on economic perspectives and interests far removed from his own. He was Daniel in the Lion's Den!

In a powerful critique of the N.A.M.'s dominant ideological commitments, Muelder wielded the sword of the World Council of Churches' idea of a responsible society (from the WCC's 1948 Amsterdam Assembly), unmasking the N.A.M.'s self-interested conception of freedom. Along the way, he sharply contrasted special interest organizations like the N.A.M. with churches with their "field" rather than "spot" values—again utilizing W. E. Hocking's distinction. We know very little about the N.A.M.'s response to Muelder's challenging words. The address does not appear to have affected the organization's policies in subsequent years. The minutes of the organization, while referring at greater length to other presentations, said only that "Dr. Muelder's address that evening recognized the contributions of American business, but emphasized that there is ample room for the improvement of business ethics." A substantial understatement!

Given the complexity of Muelder's analysis here, and its foreignness to the N.A.M.'s commitments, it may be doubted whether his listeners even understood most of this address. But its pertinence to economic realities more than 40 years later and as a striking expression of a number of themes in Muelder's ethical thought, this writing remains interesting, both for ethicists and all who share Muelder's view that economic power must be made more responsible in the contemporary world. **–JPW**

The importance of the subject to which we are asked to address ourselves is a measure of the appreciation I wish to express to the N.A.M. for the invitation to discuss it. I am highly honored to speak to you tonight and approach this theme with a sense of high seriousness, for the outcome of our discussion should be a high resolve for responsible action. We cannot help but be aware of the concern which preoccupies the minds of many thoughtful people over the general ethical condition of the social order. If we consider only those current factors that involve money in a direct way, we are appalled by the immorality of a populace that is so deeply involved in corruption, in sweepstakes, in gambling, in payola, in price-fixing, in racketeering, in graft—yes in all kinds of "dirty money" and sharp practices. These are evidences of a deep sickness rooted in personal and group selfishness and breakdown in integrity. Some of the ethical problems arise from too little competition; some from too much; some from personal defects of character; some from wrong goals; some from limited values; some from pride and power; some from inordinate love of transient good, and so on. We cannot cover the whole range of questions which involve money but must restrict ourselves to the narrower range of problems that are concerned with business in its more proper sense. I have taken as the outside guide line of topics the N.A.M. pamphlet "Industry Believes: 1962" which are policies on current problems as adopted by the board of N.A.M. They are closely related to and include "The Code of Ethics" or "Credo" of the association. I hope to make my ethical analysis of the perspectives, principles, and middle axioms found in these, leaving any precise judgments of details of business practices for another occasion. I shall refer to specific policy formulas only for purposes of illustration for more general or basic questions.

How shall I relate ethics to the policy beliefs and assumptions of business as officially held by the N.A.M.? I have noted your resolution on the clergy adopted February 7-8, 1957: "The clergy are a bulwark for fostering and preserving the spiritual values inherent in our traditional American way of life and in perpetuating the sanctity of the individual." Since you were good enough to send me the materials just referred to, I assume that these are grist for the ethical mill. Shall I approach these ethical values and beliefs in terms of a dialogue or principles? That is one familiar method of ethics. Shall I discuss the ethical context of business decisions? Shall I take a broad or narrow situational approach? There is considerable interest in that approach today. Shall I concentrate on the goals or purposes of economic life? Shall I relate the functions of an economic order to the going functions of American business and the particular policies and goals of the N.A.M.? Perhaps I shall have to indulge in each of these methods to some extent in what follows.

I

The context and perspective within which one stands when dealing with business ethics is important. It is particularly important when conversations are taking place between the clergy and organized business leaders. There is a clearly recognizable difference between the ethical context of the church and that of the N.A.M. or any other business association. The N.A.M., as its name implies, is an *association*. It exists to further the interests of its members. These interests control its policies. An association is by its nature interest-limited. These interests are implied in the Code of Business Practices and in the N.A.M. credo. Since purpose is the basic social category of all group life, the profit interests of business shape in a decisive way the limits of the various values which are acknowledged by the code and credo. A very high value is given to individual and corporation freedom in the pursuit of the profit which is necessary to the continued progress of a business. Other values are, of course, acknowledged but they are applied only to a certain point.

The context of ethical decision in which I as a clergyman stand in the ecumenical community of churches and synagogues is quite different from that of the N.A.M. The church is not an interest-limited association in the sense in which this applies to a business group. The church's inside view of itself is not that of an association at all. It is not interest-limited. The church is an organized fellowship under God with an unlimited obligation to proclaim a whole gospel for the whole man for the whole world. The purpose of the church, as H. R. Niebuhr has so simply stated it, is to increase the love of God and men in the world. To some business people this may seem to be terribly vague as compared with the concreteness of a particular business enterprise. Nevertheless, the ethical message of the church proceeds from its universal nature as church and this cannot be laid aside without violating the integrity of its mission in the world. The church's context of ethical judgment with respect to business questions is as wide as mankind's common destiny and as extended in time as both time and eternity. Every local church is the bearer of a universal gospel.

Church and business do not conduct a dialogue on the same plane or frame of reference. The church places the credo of a business association in the context of its own total responsibility for human life under God. In stating the question in this sharp way the church is not being arrogantly superior to business. I am simply recognizing the moral fact that church and business are not, despite some organizational and institutional similarities, fully comparable or congruent, and any effort to make them so will fail. There are many reasons for this, but the chief ones are that business is primarily concerned with the means of life while the church is concerned primarily with ends. Both, however, are concerned with the relations of means to ends.

Perhaps we can make this fundamental issue clearer by adopting a useful distinction made by Professor W. E. Hocking between field values and spot values. Field values are the general principles or values which provide the context for action and choice: the most general rules of the game such as justice, honesty, freedom, fair play, sportsmanship, integrity, good faith and the like. Spot values are the datable choices or experiences such as a particular business deal, a labor-management contract, the purchase of a house or car, a convention for salesmen at a particular time and place, a particular radio program, and the like. Spot values get their full meaning, not from themselves alone or primarily, but from the field values which they exemplify. In a well-ordered ethical situation the field values and the spot values will be congruent and coherent. When spot values like "success" are achieved at the expense of "field values" like justice or good faith the social order disintegrates. On the other hand, disappointments in the achievement of spot values can be tolerated if a person or the group believes that the ethical rules of the game have been observed in good faith. For example in athletic contests one team is bound to lose, but the games of the future can go on if the field values are in order. In labor-management relations some spot values will be sacrificed by some, but collective bargaining can go forward in an industry thereafter if both sides believe that the field values have been mutually respected.

Now, we must all recognize that we belong to many associations and groups. Most groups are interest-limited. This is what gives them focus and canalizes the energies of their members. Interest-limited energy makes for forward motion. A relatively narrow range of goals dominates and organizes the resources of the constituent members of an association. An association can never represent a person as a whole. The energy of an association tends to move from the many parts to a limited focus. Hence its effective power is heightened.

The church is always in danger, especially in contemporary society with its tens of thousands of associations, of becoming interest-limited like any voluntary association. When a local church or a denomination becomes legally incorporated, its officers tend to behave like those of other corporations. The incorporated church views itself as one organization with limited goals alongside other interest-limited societies. Even its theology of Christian community tends to be accommodated to its legally incorporated status. But there is a vast difference between being incorporated into Christ under the cross with a universal mission and being incorporated with limited liability under, say, the State of Delaware.

I do not object that under certain circumstances a local church incorporate. I recognize, moreover, that the business practices of many churches are poorer ethically than those of some secular business, but I am pointing out that the whole mission, witness, and service of the church can never be an interest-limited association and that the ethical contexts of the N.A.M. and of the church are therefore incommensurable. The actual interests of the entrepreneur must always be challenged by the whole range of values at stake in economic life; and it is one task of the church to keep that whole range of values before the world of business.

II

These two contrasting frames of reference are not in actual life mutually exclusive. Religion is one of the great integrative factors in society. The social order is an interacting whole. It is an interdependent system. Its dominant values tend to be pervasive. Different segments of society strive to get the values favorable to its interests to be regnant in other segments. Any major change in one part of a cultural system has profound repercussions in the others. Values interpenetrate. The economic, the political, the educational, the artistic and the religious dimensions of society are all struggling for the minds of men, and they are to a degree in competition with each other for dominance in the values held by all members of the community. Since religion is an important integrative factor in society, it tends to accommodate to the dominant values of society. In so doing it may sell its soul. The church in an industrial urban society is under pressure to define its field values so they will be congenial to business. Business would like to have the moral blessing of the church on its interpretation of field values. In its ethical mission to modern society, the church seeks to bring the goals and values of business more into line with its own vision of the Kingdom of God.

III

Let us come a little closer now to at least one dominant value of the N.A.M. and so discuss the relation of *freedom* to *responsibility*.

Freedom is a dominant theme in its code of ethics and a recurrent concept in its policy statements. "Individual freedom," the Association believes, "stems directly from God...God has given men the privilege and responsibility to pilot their own lives without undue controls or coercion." One of the Association's basic purposes is "to provide leadership in bringing about a steady improvement... in the operating of the American system of free capital and free labor so as to afford opportunity and incentive for the individual to progress and provide for the well-being and security of himself and his family." Freedom here is, of course, specifically business-limited. The N.A.M. purposes "to help create understanding of how the American free competitive enterprise system works for the benefit of every individual." Again, it says: "Effective, free and open competition is the basic regulating and directing force in our economy. It serves the public interest and provides products to consumers at the lowest possible prices." The freedom of the economy is based on the idea that "individual ambition is the most universal, reliable and powerful of human motives." "Freedom of action is based," we are told, "on individual decisions and voluntary agreements and not on commands and obedience." This means in application that "the welfare of each citizen depends primarily upon his own ability, industry and thrift. Society should not diminish "the individual's sense of responsibility for his own welfare."

When we move from the general concept of the free society and the free individual to the relation of business enterprise to government, the meaning of freedom continues to accent the minimum of external control. Thus, the idea of government competition with private enterprise is rejected. The slogan for governmental services is: "Bring government back home." All "federal collaboration in state and local responsibilities or programs should be confined to leadership through research and advice." "The Federal government has no place in an old-age assistance program." The same policy should be used in the area of protection against the costs of medical and hospital care for the aged. Policy statements consistently call for state and local action, and not federal action, in unemployment compensation and other such benefits. Freedom here means absence of restraints from federal intervention. Business also wants less restraint exercised by organized labor.

There is much that might be said in detailed response to the various principles and policies that grow out of this general view of freedom which is the pervasive theme of the statements I have just read. Some competent historians and economists would question the factual image which this vision of individual action raises. Does it correspond to the contemporary historical facts of the case?

Freedom has some significant relationship to power. Reckoned by asset values, 50 per cent of American manufacturing is held by about 150 corporations. A. A. Berle, Jr., for example, points out "that about two-thirds of the economically productive assets of the United States, excluding agriculture, are owned by a group of not more than 500 corporations. This is actual asset ownership...but in terms of power, without regard to asset positions, not only do 500 corporations control two-thirds of the non-farm economy, but within each of that 500 a still small group has the ultimate decision-making power." Though much might be made of this point, it is significant that the idea of freedom in the *credo* and policy statements of the N.A.M. does not get discussion in relation to other problems like business as a system of power. There is, however, a disclaimer that "business size, whether achieved by growth, acquisition or merger, is not in itself a criterion of undue concentration or a lack of competition." Whatever we think about this issue, it is evident that the philosophy of freedom which underlies it is rather narrowly confined and does not become a criterion of criticism of present business development.

Let us turn now, for a few moments, to the conception of the responsible society as it has been developed in the ethics of the World Council of Churches. Note in the statement which I shall read how the concept of freedom is tied organically and dialectically to the principle of responsibility in the handling of power:

"Man is created and called to be a free being, responsible to God and his neighbor. Any tendencies in state and society depriving man of the possibility of acting responsibly are a denial of God's intention for man and his work of salvation. A responsible society is one where freedom is the freedom of men who acknowledge responsibility to justice and public order, and where those who hold political authority or economic power are responsible for its exercise to God and the people whose welfare is affected by it."

The context, scope and meaning of freedom in this statement are significantly different from the business codes and policies we have just been describing. Perhaps the following commentary accents one aspect of this difference: "Man must never be made a mere means for political or economic ends. Man is not made for the state but the state for man. Man is not made for production, but production for man." Important as the idea of freedom is, it must be recognized that tensions between freedom, justice, and equality are inherent in the idea of *responsibility*. "Freedom is the freedom of men who acknowledge responsibility to justice and public order. Under modern conditions it is essential that power be distributed as widely as possible through the whole community." Those who hold economic power are responsible to God and the people whose welfare is affected by it. Such a concept avoids a doctrinaire view of freedom. On the one hand, it recognizes that there may be a constructive role which private power groups can play in society. On the other hand, it recognizes that "under many circumstances the state is the only instrument which can make freedom possible for large sectors of the population." The state is not necessarily the enemy of personal freedom and is often in complex society its guarantor. Even highly prized private property would not be conserved or defined except for the political order. Under the idea of the responsible society it might be well if the federal government intervened even more in economic life if the welfare of the people were enhanced thereby. On the other hand, it may be that business is entirely too tolerant of the federal government in developing a warfare economy.

What we need to think through is a fully responsible society. Unless we achieve a responsible society, we shall probably not be able to conserve the proper values of freedom in either economic or political life. In those parts of the economic order where relatively free enterprise has had an opportunity to develop large and powerful unities of production and management, it is by no means clear that it has conserved or enhanced individual freedom. The "organization man" is as much a business as a governmental problem. He is not, unfortunately, a complete fiction. For the white-collar worker, whether bureaucrat or manager, the crucial problem in economic life is anonymity. W. H. Ferry writes with telling force on this point:

"With the best will in the world many managers are struggling with the facelessness of corporate life...decentralization has, for example, meant more authority for more men. But company security systems and pensions and other benefits tend to lock many more into their jobs. There is, moreover, devotion to the proposition that the welfare of the employee and that of the employer are identical. There is little disagreement with Andrew Hocker's point that for a variety of reasons the corporate employee's primary commitment is to his company and not to his community or even to his own self-development." (*The Corporation and the Economy*, pp. 24-25)

IV

We must now address ourselves a little more fully to the role of the national and international political order in developing a responsible economic order.

Freedom always means a combination of liberties and restraints. The political regulations which give me liberty of access to my home restrains others from having the same access. The restraints on a company which compel safety devices on machinery give freedom from excessive danger to the worker. Laws which guarantee to workers to have unions of their own choosing put certain restraints on management. Freedom is a mixture of liberty and restraint. And the kind and amount of liberty and restraint we ought to have depends on the kind of persons we wish to develop and the kind of social order we value highly. The more national that enterprise and the market becomes the more must the legal framework of responsibility be developed and written in federal terms. It is ethically quite unrealistic to expect that a problem be dealt with effectively by a unit of political power smaller than the power that is making economic decisions. The context of decision-making must be commensurate with the situation in which the problems exist. In an age of General Motors, General Electric, General Foods and the like, it is ethically unrealistic to restrict the function of the federal government in the ways that some of the policies of the N.A.M. seem to do.

Moreover, in such an age it is ethically unrealistic to advocate the absence of union security clauses in contracts and to advocate laws which would have this absence as a federal or state policy.

Does the N.A.M. favor a degree of governmental intervention into the structure and power of unions which it opposes for its own corporation members? If the N.A.M. really believes in as much freedom from governmental intervention as possible, is it not more responsible to have union security clauses grow out of the collective bargaining process itself rather than to have laws on the state level which prevent this? What are we to think of the field values in industrial relations in states with "right-to-work" laws? Union membership as a basis of continued employment should be neither required nor forbidden by law: the decision should be left to agreement by management and labor through the process of collective bargaining. The enhancement of freedom on management's side at the expense of the loss of freedom on the side of the union casts grave reflections on the concept of freedom held by organized management. If collective bargaining is to fulfill its function in promoting industrial peace and responsibility, a corresponding legal, moral and spiritual climate—an ethos of respect—must prevail. On the whole, where unions are accepted and strong, the process of collective bargaining is mature and constructive.

Much attention has been given by the Association to the role of the federal government in the industrial field and related concerns. I was disappointed not to see a full statement on the effect of national defense industrial activity on the future welfare of the nation. The dependence of industrial activity on the economics of the Cold War should concern anyone who has real concern for freedom and the responsible society. "The defense program absorbs," according to the United States Arms Control and Disarmament Agency, "nearly a tenth of the total United States production of goods and services and employs, directly and indirectly, a like percentage of the labor force." In some industries dependence on defense employment is quite high. "Approximately 95 per cent of the employment in aircraft and missiles, 60 per cent in ship and boat building, and 40 per cent of the employment in radio and communications equipment is dependent on defense expenditures." "Defense expenditures are particularly important in precisely those industries, notably the electronics and aerospace industries, that have shown the most rapid pattern of growth and technological innovation and provided a large share of the support for research and development. The defense program now finances about half of all industrial research and development and one-fourth of all pure research." President Eisenhower's ethical concern over the power and influence of the military-industrial complex deserves more public discussion than it is receiving. I believe that anyone truly interested in freedom in our national life must concern himself aggressively with a national program of disarmament. In such a program there must be full appreciation of the planning role of the federal government and the cooperation of labor, management and government in developing a model of general and complete disarmament.

Time does not permit an adequate intrusion of these remarks to include ethical aspects of international economic relations. We can only note that the idea of the responsible society defines the unit of cooperation to be mankind as a whole. The system of sovereign nation-states is a provisional achievement which must be superseded by an adequate international political agency. Just as within the nation the problems of economic power and welfare must make business and government coherently co-ordinate, so on the international front there must be a coherent development of economic and political agencies. Most particularly at the moment the crying need is for a reconstituted United Nations organized so as to be able to carry out complete and universal disarmament. The legislative, executive, and judicial institutions of the United Nations should be strengthened so as to accomplish this end and to maintain world order. Within this framework of world-order the various national and regional economic systems could compete and co-exist. The merits of the American economy would thrive best in such a framework of disarmament and positive peace. The interest-limited freedom of the economic order might then more readily develop into a world-wide responsible society. ஐ

THE CHURCH AND THE POLITICAL ORDER

The following essay was prepared for presentation at a General Conference of The United Methodist Church on April 26, 1972. Unfortunately, the assembled delegates and bishops missed hearing it! At the top of the handwritten manuscript in the Boston archive, Muelder has written "never delivered because of tight agenda." What the intended audience missed was a lucid commentary on the perennially troubled relationship between religious bodies and the state. A life-long student of this relationship, Muelder here notes the positive importance of the state to all citizens, including Christians, but cautions against distortions.

Citing former Chief Justice Earl Warren's dictum that "law floats on a sea of ethics," Muelder stresses the importance of the churches' influence upon the culture of a society, challenging his anticipated audience to help infuse the culture with higher values and to resist baser ones. In a memorable phrase, he contrasts law floating on a sea of ethics from law floating on a sea of corruption. This theme remains as pertinent in the 21st century as it was in 1972.

While Muelder's ideas, as presented here, are not dependent upon the historical context, it is noteworthy that 1972 was a dynamic time in the nation's political history. The Vietnam War continued, despite President Nixon's having convinced the public four years earlier that he was the one who could bring it to an end. Running for re-election in 1972, the Nixon campaign was responsible for the infamous Watergate break -in and cover up which were to bring his presidency to an end two years later. Sen. George McGovern, campaigning on a clear pledge to end the war, was handicapped by a divided party and lost the election by a wide margin. His idealism, however, was in sharp contrast with the win-at-any-price campaign of his opponent.

Clearly McGovern's politics was much more in harmony with Muelder's basic ideas than Nixon's, which might raise questions about how realistic Muelder's views of the political order were. But Muelder clearly understood that the church must be in it for the long haul, anticipating significant idealistic accomplishments in the political order. One recalls Woodrow Wilson's observation that only once in a generation is a society capable of idealism in its politics. The year Muelder wrote this piece was certainly not to be that moment of idealism, but his writing remains relevant decades later. And while Muelder was anticipating delivery of this address to a United Methodist audience, his words transcend that denominational context. **–JPW**

Issues of church and state root in the relationships of religion and culture. Christianity has a long and complex involvement in the political order, with many traditions and competing doctrines that are not reconciled in the present situation. For its part, United Methodism's polity draws heavily on the American political tradition, and the debates of this General Conference reflect many of the parliamentary and extra-parliamentary devices which are commonplaces of our political life. American Methodists are a political people with deep political loyalties and sentiments which often merge and homogenize piety and politics. Even the schizophrenic Methodist...proves this, for if a champion of evangelical individualism who does not want the church to meddle in politics finds the status quo attacked, he comes to its rescue even if he uses only pietistic weapons.

The image of mixing piety and politics is a faulty image because this image assumes that two completely alien entities are thrown together externally. The cultural truth of the matter is that the political order has an ultimate dimension. The forms of politics are penultimate, and many of the institutions of politics (including the state) are earth-bound and time-bound, but such values as justice, freedom, equality, consent, responsibility and truth transcend these time-bound institutions. Persons cannot be governed without political institutions, but persons transcend all their cultural institutions. For Christians, justice is an important political value because righteousness is part of the covenant between God and persons. Freedom is an important political value because liberation is part of the redemptive work of God. Christ transcends the political order, but he sends us out to transform the political order and the whole of culture.

Religion and the political order of necessity interpenetrate, but this reality does not dispose of the problems represented in the familiar phrase, "separation of church and state." In order to clarify some of the burning issues of church and state I wish to develop a little more fully the question of religion and the public sphere, particularly the political order. No one can successfully defend the proposition that Christianity and church loyalties do not profoundly affect political life in the United States or other countries. Religious hopes and religious prejudices affect our voting, our lobbying, our protest militancy, our civil rights movement, our relations to ethnic minorities, our approach to welfare, our commitments to education, family law, taxation, and that pervasive practical heresy called civic religion. I need only to call to your minds the political influence in the General Conference of 1948 of the fact of Methodist connections of Generalissimo and Madame Chiang Kai Shek. I need only call to your mind our recent endorsement of the political activity of Bishop Muzurewa. The fact that McGovern and Wallace are both Methodists has some sectional and general political influence. Some think Billy Graham has no place in the White House, but some take the view because this seems to be a political device to keep Billy Graham devotees favorably related to the president. Others disagree with both the piety and the politics. Still others feel the president is thereby encouraging Christian living in a growing secularistic society. When Bishop Matthew Simpson was the confidant of Lincoln, Methodists were influenced thereby. During World War I, President Wilson was insistent that Anna Howard Shaw be named the head of the woman's national organization to support the war effort. The fact that she was a Methodist and the greatest woman orator of her day were, I am sure, not unimportant.

A few years ago, Chief Justice Warren noted that law floats on a sea of ethics. Unless there is a broad ethical consensus, law is in difficulty. I would extend Justice Warren's dictim as follows:

Law floats on a sea of ethics, and ethics expresses the ethos of the people. Ethics as a discipline also criticizes the ethos. There is need for both the church and the state to understand more clearly the religious source of value tensions within the democratic ethos. Because there is tension in American religion, there is strain in the democratic ethos underlying law. There are profound implications of this strain for the freedom to seek truth and to express opinions on public issues.

On the one hand, religion is a source of legitimation of law; on the other hand religion is a source of criticism of law and its administration. Society is held together by its self-enforcing values more than by force or external coercion. As R. M. MacIver said during World War II in his classic work, *The Web of Government*, the view that government rests on force is one of those half-truths that begets total error.

Now, one of the great contributions of Christianity is to feed the ethos that underlies the ethics which is the sea on which the law floats. It makes a great deal of difference what values are being fed into that sea by way of worship, education in the church-school, elementary and secondary education, the college and university, and all the voluntary societies. It matters greatly who controls and what kinds of controls are exercized on the communication of religious and moral values. It matters a great deal how firm a foundation our loyalty to Jesus Christ has laid in the practical expression of church life. If our church life is compromised by racism, by prejudice against ethnic minorities, by suburban disdain of the ghetto, by profit-seeking gain, by affluent indulgence, by status-seeking, by the cares of this world, the deceitful men or riches, and the lusts of other things, by the cocktail hour and the drug culture—then what kind of law and what kind of state can you float on that sea of pollution?

The first major point, then, of this address is that Christian churches have a responsibility for a healthy political order from the bottom of the sea of ethics to the top of the dome of government which is exerted on the ship which floats on the sea of ethics.

Two thousand years of Western history teach us the sober lesson that there are "two swords." The church is not the state and the state is not the church, but they are not isolated entities. The Constitution of the U.S.A. soundly affirmed that the state would not make any establishment of religion and that it would respect the free exercise of religion.

In the modern world, no clearer statement of the meaning of religious and civil liberty has been formulated, I believe, than the United Nation's Universal Declaration of Human Rights. "Everyone has the right to freedom of thought, conscience and religion; this right includes freedom to change his religion or belief, and freedom, either alone or in community with others and public or private, to manifest his religion or belief in teaching, practice, worship and observance." "Everyone has the right to freedom of opinion and expression; this right includes freedom to hold opinions without interference and to seek, receive and impart information and ideas through any media and regardless of frontiers."

If such values are to be conserved we need a law and a state which guarantees them. The state is not the source of these values, but it is their legal guarantor. For such values to survive they must be constantly fed into the culture out of the well-springs of faith in Jesus Christ, and they must be expressed in institutions which guarantee the freedom of the person to be fully a person. The task is wholistic, and when the church sees its task wholistically, it not only speaks about scriptural holiness but it reforms the nation. Freedom of thought, conscience and religion represent the most precious of our human rights, but these do not exist in isolation from all other human rights, and they require political institutions to guarantee them and to express them fully. If we exhibit these values in the General Conference, we feed the well springs of the truly democratic society; if we subvert these values by our conduct here, we pollute the common life and pervert the social habits of governance.

Thus far, I have spoken of freedom, but now must speak of voluntary associations. Voluntary associations are one of the glories of an open society. They are like the plankton in the ocean that release the oxygen necessary for life. The political order is not to be viewed as individual citizens at the base of the pyramid and the state at its apex, with the state having exclusive governance directly related to individual citizens. Freedom means the freedom of association. These associations number in the hundreds of thousands in our society. They make up what the Roman Catholic encyclicals celebrate in its principle of subsidiarity. They constitute family, P.T.A.s, professional societies, benevolent clubs, social clubs, art societies—thousands upon thousands of societies. These nongovernmental associations keep the social order from being closed or totalitarian or completely politicized. They are the sources of pluralism, of diversity, of dissent, of innovation. Some of them are, of course, oppressive, vicious, criminal, racist, selfish, predatory. In the words of Scripture, wheat and tares grow in the same field of voluntary associations.

Not least important as voluntary associations are the church and the private educational institution. We must therefore look at two issues: the church in relation to public and private education, and the question of taxation. Both questions cut across the older issues of church and state, for the state has a problem of taxation with respect to voluntary associations, both profit and non-profit (of which the church is one), and the state has a problem of education for the common life. Since all modern states are welfare states, the older lines of separation of church and state become inevitably blurred. How this relates to the present position which Methodist should take is not entirely clear, because we have developed no clear and consistent doctrine of the state, and our practice has often been expedient and pragmatic. Our rhetoric has often sounded like absolute separation of church and state, but our practice has often been to take public money when it was advantageous to do so. We have developed as a church no scale of priorities as to what degree of compromise is allowable in what situations. The situations are often so complex that no simplistic answers are helpful. In a rapidly changing ecumenical scene, and the secular erosion of cherished values, the financial strain on many private educational institutions has influenced a modification of attitudes.

Our social order is dual: both public and private. The public order is deeply sensitive to the desirability of voluntary societies. However, in times of crisis the state tends to be repressive with respect to voluntary associations, including churches, church-related welfare institutions, and church-related colleges. Freedom and innovation are enhanced by maintaining the dual system. The state has access to taxation. Voluntary bodies do not. It is in the interest of a democratic state to encourage healthy private institutions as well as free public ones. It is desirable to keep the system of private educational institutions alive and thriving even if this requires assistance from the public sector. It is often more economical from a taxpayer's point of view for the state to assist private institutions of learning, such as medical schools, than to allow them to collapse or to build completely new ones.

In this new situation we must be both pragmatic and have defensible guidelines. Fortunately, we can make some distinctions along the spectrum from what is intrinsically, specifically and uniquely religious and what is an expression of values so commonly held as not to raise many uniquely theological questions. There is a great deal of difference between a direct subsidy of a theological seminary and a subsidy of a medical school. There are, however, grey areas…. [*At this point, Muelder's hand-written copy ends. Presumably, in actual delivery, he would have provided a suitable conclusion.*] ☙

AUTHORITY OF CHURCH SOCIAL PRONOUNCEMENTS AND RESOLUTIONS

Throughout the 20th century, and into the 21st, mainline denominations and ecumenical bodies have issued a vast number of pronouncements on every conceivable moral issue. These range from brief resolutions adopted, almost on the spur of the moment, to lengthy position statements adopted after years of consultation. Often such statements have proved to be controversial. Christian social teaching was an important aspect of Muelder's academic life, in his teaching and writing and through his practical participation in the formulation of church positions on issues. The essay that follows was the first of three lectures on "Church Corporate Action and Personal Responsibility" which he presented to the Minnesota Annual Conference of The United Methodist Church on June 11, 1974.

His lecture could be taken as advice to all church bodies, including ecumenical councils of churches, as they address the issues of the day. It was also a more specific response to a provocative volume by Paul Ramsey challenging the authority of many ecclesial pronouncements. That book, Who Speaks for the Church?, *was Ramsey's critique of a World Council of Churches Conference on Church and Society at Geneva, Switzerland in 1966.*

Ramsey had observed that the stance taken by such church or ecumenical gatherings depends very largely on who has been invited to be present and who has not. He was, himself, present at the Geneva conference as an observer, not a delegate. Muelder's essay speaks to the authority questions posed by Ramsey, while agreeing that all church pronouncements should be preceded by careful preparation. In a brief introduction, he speaks of the authority conferred upon clergy through ordination, and afterward notes that both clergy and laity share the authority "to help write the social pronouncements of the Church and to execute them faithfully in Church and society." He then proceeds as follows: —JPW

Aperson is called of God to be a minister, and the work of an elder in the church of God is committed by the authority of the church. When the church's authority is in a state of crisis, all is in a state of crisis. With such words of authority as I have quoted, the word of the ordained ministry is related to issues of authority in society. But what of the authority that is vested in the making and carrying out of our social resolutions? It would be fair to say that there is a crisis in the authority of church social resolutions and that this crisis is part of a wider authority crisis of the church. When a person is baptized or ordained, that person is baptized or ordained or admitted into the full fellowship of the church, not only in The United Methodist Church but in the whole church of God.

The crisis of social pronouncements is an ecumenical one. And the crisis of authoritative church social resolutions is part of the ecumenical crisis, both internally and externally.

Internally it includes the dimension of renewal, reform and change necessary to every church, and externally it includes the church's outward orientation to and for the world. This two-fold crisis holds for the Roman Catholic Church or the Orthodox Churches and for Protestants alike. To be pastorally and prophetically effective at the present time has become a tensional problem between being radically Christian, on the one hand, and adaptive to modern society and the world's cultures on the other.

A good and sound social pronouncement partakes of the internal crisis of authority and of the external orientation in society. In one sense, the question of the authority of our pronouncements is an institutional one at a time when individualism and pluralism are right. In 1967, following the Geneva Conference on Church and Society held by the World Council of Churches, Paul Ramsey raised some basic questions in a book called, *Who Speaks for the Church?* We shall examine some of his important theses about how specific the church's social resolutions should be, and still be authoritative in a Christian sense. It is possible to be Christian in a certain sense and not be relevant, and it is possible to be relevant and not Christian.

For the moment, I wish to accent the fact that, in all parts of the ecumenical movement, the crisis of authority is one of self-understanding within the church as a theological and as a social institution. In his fine book, *The Interaction of Law and Religion*, Professor Harold Berman of the Harvard Law School observes:

"The crisis of religion in America today does not arise as it did in Luther's time from its excessive legalization; on the contrary, it is the decline in the institutional self-identification of religion and in its social forms of expression; it is the weaknesses of the church as formal communities—that is a principal symptom if not a principal cause of the impotence of Christianity today. Religion in America is becoming the private affair of individuals seeking to be unburdened of their loneliness, the cult of personal peace of mind...In these circumstances, religionless Christianity only contributes to the danger of new Christianity-less religions—political and social faiths—which lack all conviction or, even worse, are only full of passionate intensity."[22]

Christianity claims to be the Word of God, a Divine Word, within history. But how many persons attending, voting on—for or against, reporting back home, and seeking to carry out a resolution, have a sense that these social resolutions are an expression or extension of that Divine Word in contemporary history?

The problem, we say, is hermeneutical; that is, it is one of interpretation. And Scripture is itself not revelation but interpretation of revelatory events. As one Catholic scholar puts it: "The interpretative function to proclaim the Word with contemporary vitality and with historical veracity must realize itself in each era so that neither existential situation nor sovereign gospel is slighted."[23]

The writing of social resolutions participates in this ongoing re-interpretation of the church in its life and ministry to and for the world. Such events as black theology, women's theology and liberation theology, all participate in this interpretive crisis. Who speaks with authority means, in part, who interprets convincingly what the Holy Spirit is now saying to the churches and to the world? The social, ethical elements in these movements are crucial,

---

22. Nashville: Abingdon Press, 1974, pp. 95-96.
23. Thomas Franklin O'Mera, O.P., "Is There a Common Authority for Christians?", *The Ecumenical Review*, 22 (Jan., 1970), p. 19f.

for they deal with oppression; and, consequently, a sound view of theology is imperative if the social pronouncements are to be authoritative. And it is a problem not only for a piece of the church; it is a problem for the whole church.

"Political theology," as liberation theology is sometimes called, may bring the Christian community to a new intensity. It may be a response to the social consciousness of the times, and it may be part of the renewal of the church. But great social pronouncements, taken as theological statements relevant for action, are never explicable alone in terms of the political or economic social process or the secular crisis. All sound theology is answerable to the whole church and should result from it as a complex organism and institution.

THE PROBLEM IS to find and to express the normative mind of the whole church in relation to the general conscience of mankind. Social pronouncements are a problem when they do not express a defensible interpretation of the Gospel. Like all authoritative statements, they should help the present generation to retrieve the Gospel message. They should preserve that message in the present life of the church, and they should help lead the church in its mission. So interpretation, authority and leadership go together in a dialectical interaction. The God of history gives the church a mission whose constant renewal requires interpretative leadership.

Quite definitely, the crisis of authority is a crisis of leadership. Some regard it as a crisis of loyalty and obedience to tradition. But, even more, it is a crisis of permanent renewal of responsible leadership. Pronouncements, however valid as propositions, have authority only as moral elements when they are put into operation. If we do not lead the church with the social pronouncements we have, the social pronouncements become dead letters, and they lose their authority.

One group, the first group I shall discuss of such variables, may be designated as sociological. Under this heading would come impatience with history and tradition in a period of rapid social change. Traditional fields, however meritorious intrinsically, are regarded as irrelevant. Then there is the relativism that arises from competing claims to ultimate truth. Nothing is more conducive to skepticism than the conflicts of absolute claims. Two hundred-fifty or 350 rival denominations all claiming to be absolutely right cannot possibly be authoritative. One aspect of this relativism is the sheer number of pronouncements on modern problems. This is also a problem for United Methodists. If we pronounce too many times on too many things, everything cancels out or relativizes all the other things.

Once the Methodist Church could publish its own statements all in the Discipline. Of late, the clamor is for a separate book of resolutions.[24] Another aspect of this is the frequently divided vote between clergy and laity on major problems of economic order and the question of race, of war, of peace and of women's liberation. Another is the confusion between study and consultative conferences and legislative assemblies with delegated representatives. Often conferences that are called to study a question end up by passing resolutions and thus want to be action conferences. Often the desire to do something is so strong that a study conference becomes an occasion to make action-oriented pronouncements. This is a serious error. This impulse is related to the often misunderstood difference between speaking *to* the church, which is a study conference, and speaking *for* the church, which are legislative conferences. Statements or findings that are drafted to inform and guide further study process in the church are often publicized as findings of the church and tend to create a breakdown in authority.

Still another sociological factor is the struggle between liberals and conservatives for the control of the legislative process and for dominating the parliamentary situation. If one side wins, it thinks the church has won. May be it has; sometimes it hasn't. I am listing this political struggle as sociological because it bears not on the normative quality of church statements but on the setting in which they are made and the manner in which they are achieved. Authority declines when social pronouncements are not reinforced

---

24. Editor's note: Shortly after this, The United Methodist Church did begin publishing a separate *Book of Resolutions*, and at the end of the 20th century that volume had grown to nearly a thousand pages, nicely illustrating the problem Muelder has raised here.

by proper administration or are not defended vigorously. In The United Methodist Church, this sometimes happens in the boards and agencies, sometimes in the Council of Bishops, sometimes at the local conference level and, often, because of their being ignored in the local church. The only way to defend the Social Creed is to apply it. That is its authority. Not to act and lead when the issue is joined is to weaken the meaning and the power of the creed. Let us not forget that, unlike the state, the churches' enforcement powers are limited in their sanctions, but they should not default on the moral power they have. They are able to inform, to motivate, to guide, and above all to speak with the authority of the Gospel.

Another group of variables arises out of the knowledge situation, what one might call the epistemological dilemma. Today there is a general posture that "certainty" is impossible to achieve and that there are only varying degrees of "certitude." So there is a general skeptical posture towards all statements. Both modern science and modern philosophy stress the failure of the quest for certainty, yet some devotees of science are themselves guilty of scientism. They feel that scientific statements have priority over all other statements. At a conference on ethics and bio-technics, I heard a scientist say, dealing with a genetic problem: "When the biological problem has been solved, the theological problem goes away.

ANOTHER SET OF PROBLEMS arises from theology and the way theology is practiced in the making of our pronouncements. We may cite, first, the lack of unity in the church. This scandalous lack of unity is both a cause and a consequence of the breakdown of authority. There are the theological conflicts which still separate the churches and distinguish churches from sects. There is the general lag of conservative church values behind the cultural developments that attend scientific and theological possibilities. Illustrations are: integrity of the body today, the ontic reality of the person, the problems arising from the Skinnerian control of behavior, which seems to assert that the main thing is to control behavior of people, not to convert or persuade their minds, to mention only a few. Then too, theological appeals to the authority of Scripture have contributed both to the authority of church resolutions and to the decay of authority, depending upon how the authority of the church is used and how the Scripture is employed.

Theological appeals in ethics, primarily now to one and now to another member of the Trinity, also affect this matter of authority. When the appeal is to the authority of God the Father, the outcome may be based on some classical natural law, or overall philosophical principle, or the ordering of creation, or the mandates of creation, as they are sometimes called. Or to God as process, or to natural theology or some other form of philosophical theology. These may all be very important and valid. I'm not negating them. I'm simply pointing out how we sometimes go about theological work in formulating social statements. When the appeal to revelation is to the authority of Christ the Son, the stress is less on law and order, or justice, or principle, or reason, or universals or on divine providence, and it is more on love, redemption, reconciliation, the covenant of grace, and the church as the extension of Christ. In short, we often get *koinonia* or community ethics. And when the appeal is to the Holy Spirit, the authority of the Holy Spirit, the resolutions are even more anti-legalistic. They are more charismatic. They tend to be more innovative, situational, anti-institutional, and even antinomian. Hence, we may argue that the theological aspects of social pronouncements, to be truly normative and to be truly persuasive, should appeal to the Godhead as a whole; they should be truly Trinitarian, and they should square with what we hold as true about God as Father, God as Son, and God as Holy Spirit. Otherwise we may feed one or another tendency that is in conflict with the whole truth.

IN 1972, POPE PAUL VI criticized the intention of some to dissolve the teaching authority of the church, either by equivocal pluralism, conceived as a free interpretation of the doctrine of the church, and the unchallenged co-existence of opposing ideas, or by a subsidiarity which is intended to be autonomy. And certainly no one knows more about the crisis of authority right now than Pope Paul VI.

A fourth group of variables that makes for the decline of authority of social pronouncements, I shall group under the general heading, "Secularism and Sin." Besides the errors of scientism are the corrosive effects of the general secularism of our culture and the worldliness that is in the church. Many church people resist ethical statements because they challenge their comfortable living, their irresponsibility and their present privileges. There is in the church a decline in the moral sense of sin. A studied and habitual sensitivity to the unity of mankind, to the great ranges of inequality in our society, is the root cause of displeasure with radical propositions. Many people do not like controversial statements. People who do not like controversial statements are usually in a state of sin.

Agencies of the church, including hospitals, sometimes repudiate responsibility for mankind as a whole. Attacks on the church's authority in social questions sometimes comes from the conviction that the church is intermeshed with institutions that have outlived, if they ever truly served, their time.

And when the church supports social values which have become widely discredited, its moral stature is diminished. Moreover, in times of deep divisions, such as we are having today, men and women do not ask for the condemnation of all injustices, but only of those that have been committed by their opponents. Disunity is thus a central and corrosive force in social ethics. What needs to be retained in all such situations is a deep sense of the transcendent element in Christianity. "My kingdom is not of this world," said Jesus. There are many ways of interpreting it, but in its context it had a very important element. It can be interpreted as an other-worldly statement, but it may also call attention to the fact that there is no simple identification possible between the Kingdom of God and any positive social policy or practice, however attractive. The Kingdom of Christ does not prescribe the political and social regulations under which people must live in every detail. "It is true," says Bishop Vaughan, "that Christendom was an attempt to translate Christianity into social and cultural terms, but the collapse of the medieval experiment has not destroyed the Christian faith itself."

Somehow, there was a sufficiently transcendent element in the Christian faith to survive medieval Christianity. "It has simply revealed the contingent nature of all attempts to express Christianity in a particular cultural form...Christianity can live within a secular state without violence to its essential nature," but it must be faithful to itself. The transcendent element is not only a resource, but it is also a source of legitimate relativity. Thus, one reason, as noted above, that church pronouncements lose their authority is the intermeshing of the church with institutions that have outlived their usefulness. At the same time the transcendent element in the Kingdom makes it available for a new expression of relevance, when it has found its own self-identity as distinct from the institutional embodiments it formerly had taken.

THE TRANSCENDENT ELEMENT is also functional in providing the basis for the church and its message to be supranational and as universal as mankind in all its complex pluralism of culture and civilization. It may very well be that one of the greatest contests of our time is the conflict between a genuine Christianity and civic religion, which is a mixture of civic life and practice and Christianity. It is hard to sort this out at times, but it is essential to do so. Yet, in Christ the transcendence is historical. Christ is not only transcendent, he is historically incarnate. Our actions and interpretations are also in history. In an exchange between Kung and Rahner, two of the great Catholic theologians, back in 1971, one reads this statement: "If the truth is historical then the truth of a doctrine cannot be fulfilled simply by repeating it." To protect and promote the truth, the doctrine must again and again be reinterpreted in the church's on-going history. It is important that social pronouncements make plain what that transcendent element is, as well as what the historically relevant in the pronouncement is.

Now I should like to turn briefly to another aspect of our authority problem, the way our pronouncements are made. Most social pronouncements are enacted or passed by legislative assemblies and, therefore, appeal to parliamentary authority. And, to put it very briefly, we sometimes do not sort out theological authority from parliamentary authority. Political authority is often approved or rejected, but it enters into the making and establishing of many social resolutions. The authority of a governing body may be defined as the right to command and direct, to be heard or obeyed by others. This right is voluntarily accepted by the people and exists without the imposition of sanctions. The power of an assembly is derivative, and its authority is invested by those who created the assembly. We stress here the sense of moral obligation which the people have in experiencing governmental authority. Four considerations enter into this feeling of moral obligation on our part with respect to legislative assemblies, both in the church and outside it. And if they are all present, the sense of the authority of those statements or actions is strong. If they are weak in certain aspects, the feeling of obligation is diminished.

First, there is a belief that the assertion of power through legislation is for the common good of society. Here we may distinguish further between the sense of serving the common good in a general way and the particular good which is at stake in the legislation under consideration.

Second, when there are supra-human factors believed in that are involved in the legislation, authority is enhanced. Here we may note the agreements in theological belief or interpretation. Resolutions that are closer to the traditional nuclear beliefs of the assembly carry a greater sense of moral obligation than those which are transiently secular in the desacralized sense of secular. Or, in another sense, new issues carry with them less sense of authority when acted on than issues which are already deeply rooted in the conscience of the church. Thus, we must expect to have much more controversy on new issues than on those with which the church has dealt over the years and in many situations.

A third element is the legitimacy of the resolutions owing to their source or issuer. Here we must consider the various sources of legitimacy, including the procedures whereby legislation is drafted, processed and adopted. Many doubts are expressed from time to time because resolutions are regarded as non-representative in a parliamentary sense or have been hastily drafted or inadequately debated, and the like. One can sometimes get propositions through an assembly and seem to have scored a great victory; and yet many go back home without a sense that the actions have any authority over them. There are no short cuts, really, to authority.

A fourth source of a sense of moral obligation is conformity to our accepted norms. This may involve the explicit norms or the underlying ethos beneath these norms. Resolutions are extensions of the cumulative body of convictions and the evident expression of the unifying body of values. These have much greater authority than those which, however rational in themselves, depart from these common elements that are found in the community that is organized for parliamentary purposes. Many scholars believe that the principal contribution of the church is to the underlying ethos rather than to rules and legislation. Political authority is not the same as theological authority or moral authority, but political authority is enhanced when theological and moral authority underlie the enactments. There is much displeasure when parliamentary procedures are followed in form but not in spirit.

Often, even good parliamentary process is not adhered to in church conferences and assemblies. Paul Ramsey has some telling arguments against many of the resolutions which are passed by church bodies because they violate fair political process. And I must agree, after attending hundreds of these meetings across the years, that the process in Annual Conference and General Conference often resembles a leapfrogging from one major resolution to another without benefit of sufficient deliberation in between.

Following the 1966 World Study Conference on Church and Society, Ramsey, as I mentioned above, wrote a vigorous book entitled, *Who Speaks for the Church?* It was a one-sided critique of the Geneva Conference and of the methods and goals of the World Council of Churches, the National Council of Churches, and their member denominations when they deal with urgent social and political questions. He did not address the authority question as such, but aspects of it are involved in his attack. He said, "I mean the passion for numerous particular pronouncements on policy questions to the consequent neglect of basic decisions and action-oriented principles of ethical and political analysis."[25] I think what

---

25. Ramsey, p. 13.

he is trying to get at is the following: We do have our general overall theological convictions. We get terribly concerned about a specific social issue and crisis in our community or the nation, and we direct ourselves to this. But we have not always developed these intermediary propositions which form the moral bridge between the ultimate theological convictions and the precise social policy which agitates us for consideration at the moment. He was hoping to reverse the tendency, and I feel he went too far, of trying to reach agreement upon specific pronouncements or conclusions. He found this misleading and oppressive to the conscience of many sincere Christians. He questioned the penchant for such specific resolutions, particularly when the church hardly knew its own mind or had a common mind on the basic principles assumed in these statements. He advocated the following: "Radical steps need to be taken in ecumenical ethics if ever we are to correct the pretense that we are makers of political policy and get on with our proper task of nourishing, judging, and repairing the moral and political ethics of our times."[26] One has to address the problem at a different level.

His criticism has a two-fold focus. First, when directions for decisions are given, they often have too few Christian warrants. And second, the hurry to commit the church to particular pronouncements is a danger. This is rather, he thinks, the proper work of secular prudence, not of church bodies. At this point I do not agree.

In such a major criticism, the question of authority involves the nature, purpose and role of the church. That is: "What is its mission in today's society?" Speaking of the Geneva Conference he pressed for sounder deliberating processes. I may interject that compared with most General and Annual Conference preparatory studies, the legislative processes of the World Council of churches have been models of deliberation. But when compared with Vatican II, they are all lacking in the maturing process of deliberation prior to adoption. What great church body, apart from the Roman Catholic Church, has spent four years of about three months

---

26. *Ibid.*

of each year to updating its relation to the modern world? What came out is really worthy of all of that effort. But what is at stake in Ramsey's critique is not only the competence of deliberation. The goal itself is under review. He says: "The aim of these procedures and deliberations should not be to improve the church's speaking to the world its supposedly expert specific advice, but to make sure that in everything addressed to the churches and to the world to-day, our Church Councils can better speak *for* the church, for the *whole* Christian truth, and every saving word, but not more than can be said on such a basis."[27]

What should be said in reply to the issues raised by Ramsey? Ramsey's view tends toward a conservative and even static view of the church in history, one in which the actor is able at all times to touch all bases before taking a fresh position, one which stresses the institution as established more than as the church in pilgrimage. When we are in pilgrimage, we must run risks.

MUST WE HAVE FULL theological consensus before we can act on questions of social ethics? John Bennett does not think so. He does not think that the church should wait until there is a common position in the church beyond all significant debate. Given our evident pluralistic situation in theology, established traditions, varieties of interpretation and various schools of theological thought, it is not realistic to expect much in the way of specific resolutions if we wait for full prior agreement on our theological beliefs. There is such a thing as having an immature theological posture. But immaturity aside, the church must run risks in the positions it takes if it is to fulfill its mission and take its own ultimate beliefs seriously. To be sure, procedures must be sought that avoid snap judgments, misinformation, technical incompetence and manipulative partisanship. But a church that never risks specific judgments may be charged with not seriously meaning what it says. The meaning of ideas is exposed in the actions they lead to. To remain at high abstract theological levels is to invite not being taken seriously.

---

27. *Ibid.*, p. 43.

I do not doubt that the dispatch of hundreds of resolutions in the course of a few days and weeks weakens the effective authority of the church. Ramming through the legislative process scores of important proposals in the closing sessions of an assembly is generally a social ethics horror story. When this is done, the formal authority of the legislative assembly is undermined by the violence done to the processes of reasoned consent. If we are to have voluntary consent, it must be informed consent; and it must be genuine consent. On much Methodist legislation we are, unfortunately, often in the above situation. There seems to be a compulsion to be relevant on all conceivable issues that all Methodists can possibly bring to a legislative assembly. This, I think, we must get past.

In summary now, we can make a number of general observations about the problem of authority in our social pronouncements. First, to be authoritative, social pronouncements must embody persuasive ethical merit. It is not sufficient that they have legislative legitimacy. Their theological and ethical merit must have a different order of validation than skillful parliamentary processing. They must interpret what can be recognized as the moral conscience of humanity in the light of the Gospel.

Secondly, social Christianity's long tradition through the Social Creed, the World Ecumenical Conferences and the idea of a responsible society has penetrated the churches sufficiently to provide an ethos to which many social pronouncements can appeal. To a significant degree there exists a united and coordinated vision of problems and ideals. But this vision and the sense of responsibility have not yet achieved the same authority on recent problems as on older problems; that is, those arising from the bio-technical revolution in biology, medicine and issues of life and death.

Third, there is a growing sense of recognition of a common responsibility for and a common destiny of man and society. As never before in history, I think we do recognize that all of mankind has one destiny that is morally a unity. At the same time, there is a strong feeling in the churches of Asia, Africa and Latin America that the Western churches have not perceived and do not yet perceive correctly the specific needs and values of those indigenous churches and of the cultures in which they are located. We must give this concern our attention.

Fourth, there is a growing acceptance of the vocation of missions and of the expectation that the church is an agent of change as well as of conservation. Mission means innovation. Innovation is disruptive. Conflict has biblical authorization. We simply have to live with it. It belongs to our life.

Fifth, Methodism's social resolutions have a greatly mixed authority. They are not all equally authoritative and do not all equally deserve the same authority. Some have deep rootage in the social interpretation and others present themselves as not very matured and even as rather ad hoc. Methodism's pronouncements on the whole have not been based on a coherent social ethic but have been made one at a time, often in quite pragmatic situational encounters, and somewhat inconsistently with each other. We need to bring greater theological and moral coherence to our statements as a whole.

Sixth, the struggle to find an authoritative social ethic appropriate to a supra-national Christian community cannot be resolved by making inductions from innumerable resolutions passed by legislative assemblies. What I mean is that the solution is not to take our *Book of Resolutions* and to deduce out of the innumerably large number of resolutions we have passed what the overall ethic should be. The making of social pronouncements is not an inductive matter. It is the problem of finding moral coherence and theological coherence of the Gospel in relationship to contemporary lives.

And finally, coming back to one of the first points, the crisis of authority is a crisis of leadership. This means that the authority of social pronouncements depends on the vigorous thrust of leadership in times of crisis as an expression of the mission of the church. The authority [of leaders] is therefore more pastoral than dogmatic. It depends, more than bishops, pastors and laypersons usually recognize on the right word spoken as a living word at the right time with courage. This right word spoken at the right time influences the moral environment in which secular positions in our society are formulated. Done consistently and throughout the church they can change the moral climate of America—which greatly needs changing. ☜

Conclusion

The Legacy of Walter G. Muelder

AN APPRECIATIVE CRITIQUE

The Personalist as a Person

Before offering a few thoughts about the intellectual legacy left by Walter G. Muelder, I wish to record some observations about him as a person. After assuming a pastorate, rather late in my career, I began to notice something about the funerals or memorial services at which I was asked to officiate. Almost invariably, in speaking of the one who had died, some particular note, often a particular passage from Scripture, seemed to summarize the meaning of this person's life. It was as though everything had finally come together, and people looking back upon that life, could now see it whole.

In the case of Walter Muelder, one can fairly ask whether his philosophy and theology of personalism fit his own life as a person. My own response to that is to say "yes," emphatically. Nothing about his life contradicted his philosophy. Indeed, to borrow one of his and Brightman's favorite words, his life was *coherent* with his thought! He would say that his life was a personally lived form of "emergent coherence." Which is to say that the longer he lived, the more factors had to be and were integrated. I am struck by the testimony of Dr. Asare, included in the Introduction to this book, about the warm hospitality the Muelders showed him and his family and how easy it was for him to become a pastor to this great teacher. Muelder was gifted with a superb mind, but he understood that first he was human. I won't linger over how rare that is among people who have such intellectual gifts! Special moments leap to mind, such as this one: After the conclusion of my doctoral oral dissertation defense in 1960, he accepted my invitation, offered on the spur of the moment, to have lunch with my wife and me in our nearby apartment, dropping everything else to share that special time with us and to make over our infant son, Stephen. He was to be a real friend for the rest of his life. And, at various turns in my own career, I found him an invaluable source of counsel—never dominating, always generous and wise.

There were, of course, some foibles. I still chuckle over a lunch we had together well after he had turned 90. He proudly announced to me that he had just had his Massachusetts driver's license renewed. Seeing what must have been a look of horror on my face, he hastily added that of course he only drove in the neighborhood of his retirement home. Other than that, he relied upon friends, including his long-time colleague, Paul Deats. And I can recall, with good humor, the way he protected his time in a very busy schedule by holding his watch, quite visibly, while in conference with loquacious graduate students like me. But, even under pressure of time, he could be warmly gracious and thoughtful. He could present a forbidding exterior to many students. In time, I came to see that there was an innate shyness in his disposition; certainly it was not a judgmental attitude. And put alongside that his great generosity with his time and energy. And much, much more: put it alongside his patient, tender care of his wife Martha in her declining years, when he performed even the most menial tasks without complaint.

Quite apart from anything he wrote or lectured, his was a life well lived.

Enduring Insights

A number of the base points in Muelder's thinking, including those singled out in the Introduction, represent enduring contributions to Christian ethics. Muelder makes few claims to originality. Indeed, his ethical method always emphasized our need to rely upon the work of others. In the introduction to his *Foundations of the Responsible Society,* he writes that

"…in some respects my argumentation may appear quite eclectic, but there is an intention to go beyond a mosaic of borrowed concepts to a new level of interdisciplinary integration. At the same time I wish students especially to be aware of the vast range of specialized literature in many fields which bear on social ethics. I am here writing, as I always work, at the intersectional points of theological, philosophical and social science disciplines, aware of their varied and often conflicting traditions of methodology and conceptions of truth."

There is no apology here for being "eclectic." One can almost hear him criticizing some practioners of the field for their excessive claims to originality, especially when this involves the creation of new intellectual fads. In the end, we are always borrowing. But, as he notes in this same quotation, we are still pushing toward new levels of interdisciplinary integration or a better synthesis. Expertise in ethics includes, perhaps at its center, proficiency in making the connections. And since our knowledge is never complete, neither are the connections.

That point is especially apparent in the often elusive effort to connect norms with facts. It is not always so easy to know, with certainty, how to embody the ultimate good in the real world, and a number of the most troubling moral controversies of our time are joined at exactly that point. Take, for instance, the question of homosexuality that has vexed the churches and wider public for decades. What is it, really? Why is it that some people are homosexual in orientation and others hetrosexual—and some in between? Would it matter if there were very clear scientific evidence that sexual orientation is altogether genetic in causation? Or that it is purely a matter of how one has been nurtured? Or that it is a result of particular relationships or choices of lifestyle? Then there is the question whether it even matters very much. What can be known, factually, about the lives of gay and lesbian people? Are they more or less "functional," psychologically and socially, than other people? If they are shown to be "normal" by accepted views of what that means, does that mean that there is nothing morally objectionable about gay and lesbian relationships? And does it matter whether these relationships are monogamous or promiscuous? One can see here an array of factual questions, the answers to which cannot be supplied simply by intuition or pre-judgment.

Likewise, the controversies over abortion. Once it is granted that killing infants is to be condemned and made subject to criminal law, there is the factual question of the status of prenatal life. Is a fetus to be regarded as a person? An answer to that question would seem to hinge, in large measure, on what are the biological characteristics of personhood? Is it the DNA itself, and if so, why? Is it the nervous system and brain, and if so at what stage of development? Further factual questions of great importance have to do with the effects upon the woman of carrying or not carrying a pregnancy to term, or the effects upon a family economically and relationally. And there is the yet further factual question of anticipated consequences if abortion were prohibited in criminal law.

Economic issues, too, raise both normative and factual questions. If we believe, as Muelder does, that humanity is intended by God to be one moral community of love and justice, one of the most important factual questions is how to undergird this normative vision economically. How can we ensure that people receive the food, clothing, shelter and medical care needed to sustain life and enable participation in community? How can we structure economic life so that huge disparities of income and wealth do not create barriers within community, even when everybody has enough of the economic necessities to sustain life and health? How, within economic life, can we provide vocational opportunity so that all can make their creative contributions to the common good? Such questions, which have taxed philosophers and theologians and ethicists from time immemorial, require convincing factual answers.

Such questions are raised with special urgency in global terms. On the one hand, billions of the world's people live at or below subsistence levels, even as the United States and Canada, Europe and Japan enjoy unprecedented prosperity. On the other hand, the rapid expansion of a world market threatens to undermine the well-being of American and European workers, even as cheap labor in underdeveloped countries can lead to exploitation. Advocates of the various free-trade agreements promise increased trade and greater prosperity for all, while critics fear deeper divisions within the God-intended world community of love and justice. The situation cries out for the most careful kinds of economic research that are not distorted by ideological pre-judgments of either "right" or "left." The ultimate goals of economic life are in the normative sphere; the means to achieve those goals are largely empirical.

Numbers of other illustrations could be presented, demonstrating the importance of careful factual study in concert with thoughtfully expressed moral objectives. It is beyond our purposes here to examine these problems in contemporary life. But it should be evident that Muelder is exactly right in affirming the importance of the physical and social sciences. It is not that science can provide us with the norms, but the scientific disciplines can be enormously important in placing the norms in factual context. Science, when not subsuming the roles of philosophy or theology, is disciplined pursuit of factual truth. It is getting at those factual questions in an orderly way. Serious work in social ethics cannot be pursued rigorously without that taking the sciences into account. We can thank Walter Muelder for relentlessly telling us that that is so.

The Personalistic Vision

We can also thank him for the way he appropriated Boston Personalism into his own thinking. Sometimes earlier 20th century Personalism was presented in more sterile, abstract form—or so it seemed to Boston students, myself included. It was an idealistic philosophy, its truths presented and argued in propositional form. There is a place for that. But there is also irony, for if there is anything that is *not* an abstract proposition, it is a real *person*! The concept of person points toward that reality, but it cannot embody it. That requires a different kind of rhetoric and a whole lot more illustration. Somehow, Muelder's writing, and above all his teaching, was able to bring that kind of life to the subject.

 In part that was because of his emphasis upon love as the central point in theology. With Muelder, love is neither an abstraction nor sentimental. It is good will, in the Kantian sense, and an expression of *koinonia*, the love binding us together in community—an understanding he shared with his theological colleague, L. Harold DeWolf. It is what makes personhood a living reality. Muelder would not claim that the centrality of love was anything original with him, and yet the way he integrated this with his philosophical/theological personalism is striking. Love is in the heart of the Christian gospel, rhetorically expressed in the Sermon on the Mount, redemptively and sacrificially expressed by Christ on the cross. This emphasis upon love also reveals Muelder's deeply Methodist heritage, for that was absolutely central to John Wesley. But of course even Wesley could lay no claim to originality at that point.

In Muelder's ethic, love is essentially central to his commitment to pacifism. I shall have more to say on that subject later, but whatever one may think about the adequacy of pacifism as an overall stance in this-world conflicts, the pacifist position is a ringing affirmation of the power of love in human life. I cannot conceive of a Christian ethic that is not based upon the centrality of love. There have been different ways of stating and applying this in Christian ethics, including Luther's "strange work of love" that is distinctly not pacifist. But Muelder's pacifist vision unquestionably rises out of a deep grasp of the centrality of love in all Christian ethics.

In one of his more autobiographical writings, Muelder expresses some surprise that "critics sometimes charged me with having no theology" (*The Ethical Edge of Christian Theology*, p. 33). His response is to note that these critics should have taken more account of the seminary context in which he served as well as his participation in preparations for ecumenical conferences. A better response would be to refer any such critics to his actual writings and to note the way in which he could move seamlessly between philosophy or philosophical theology and systematic theology. Any of his students could attest to that as well. But, perhaps the deeper issue is that some of his critics themselves lacked the capacity to make translations between philosophy and theology. That is, in the end, the question of whether it is possible for theology to face the truth question honestly. We can be grateful to Muelder for doing so and thereby helping to model how this can be done through a refined version of the personalistic philosophy. His refinements, in which he moved beyond his great mentor Edgar S. Brightman, were at two points: "(1) toward a historical communitarian view of human personality and (2) toward a much larger use of empirical social sciences" (see his *Ethical Edge*, p. 6). Both of these were points setting the stage for his lifetime concentration on social ethics.

BEYOND MUELDER

In a certain sense, as we have noted, Muelder expected all se-rious students to move beyond their teacher. The role of a great teacher, which he understood full well, is to lay foundations; the quest for truth, theological and otherwise, is an never-ending task. That may be especially true of ethics, for the ongoing parade of new problems and issues is relentless. What about the movement beyond Muelder?

Principles and Relationships

We can begin with the moral laws. Muelder was deeply influ-enced by Brightman's book, *Moral Laws,* which, I believe, he was acquainted with even in the writing process while he and Bright-man were both in Germany. The formulation of moral laws in that volume was prominent in some of Muelder's classes and in his own book, *Moral Law in Christian Social Ethics* (John Knox Press, 1966). Muelder, in company with L. Harold DeWolf, had expand-ed the Brightman list of principles to include the communitar-ian dimension more directly. I myself made substantial use of the "moral laws" in my Ph. D. dissertation on "A Strategy for Racial Desegregation in The Methodist Church" (published in 1960 by Boston University Press and Public Affairs Press), and I found the principles quite useful in business ethics seminars conducted for corporate leaders in the early 1960s. As stated by Brightman and, in refined form, by Muelder, each of the principles is self-evidently valid. For example, the rule of the "Best Possible," that we should always aim at doing the best possible, or the "Law of Consequenc-es," that we should foresee and approve the consequences of our actions. Who could object?

Perhaps nobody should. It is not unusual for people to think about ethics as rules to govern behavior. We may not obey the rules governing right and wrong, but conscience inflicts a sense of guilt upon us when we do not. And if ethics comes down to rules of right behavior, the moral laws set forth by Brightman and refined by Muelder and DeWolf seem almost self-evidently valid. This is what ethicists would describe as a prescriptive view of ethics: rules or principles that have been prescribed.

But there are other ways of viewing ethics. H. Richard Niebuhr and Edward LeRoy Long, Jr., remind us that ethics can also be framed in terms of the good to be sought. This is what ethicists describe as a "consequentialist" ethic—one that focuses on consequences. Of course, the moral law tradition has its "law of consequences" that sounds very much like that, but the focus there is more upon obeying the law than on identifying and seeking the good for its own sake. And then, ethics can be understood in terms of loving relationships. Indeed, that would appear to be the deeper import of personalism itself—that we should find fulfillment through loving relationships with God and other people and not through being right.

Do these other ways of looking at ethics negate the Moral Laws? I do not think so. Each of these three approaches to ethics—rules or principles, consequences, and relationships—contribute important dimensions to our understanding. But it may make a difference which of these is primary. If love is, indeed, the centerpoint of Christian ethics, then any rules or principles are for the sake of love and not the other way around.

Love and the Quest for Peace with Justice

I have rarely disagreed with my old mentor on anything, through the years. Probably the most important point of disagreement has been with his pacifism. Having been a pacifist myself during my college years, I came to believe that there had to be some moral ground for resisting evil with lethal force, when necessary. So I found the "just war" tradition more compatible with my views, particularly as I made use of its criteria in evaluating, and rejecting, the U.S. war in Vietnam. Muelder's pacifism was, in fact, not without a touch of irony. It would seem that the moral law of the "best possible" and the law of "consequences" are much closer to the just war tradition than to the absolutes of pacifism. What if, in light of foreseeable *consequences*, military action is the *best possible* way to do the loving thing under particular historical circumstances? Would the failure by the international community to intervene militarily in Rwanda and Burundi, in order to save hundreds of thousands of lives, illustrate the point? We can't be entirely sure, of course, for history does not disclose its alternatives, the nature of events that never happened. Muelder could and did argue that non-violent alternatives to lethal force can, in the end, produce better consequences than the military alternatives. My impression is that his pacifism was primarily a rejection of conflict between and among nations; he seemed more open to the necessary use of force when responsible to a legitimate authority. Thus, the local police (who should still practice great restraint) could use force in behalf of maintaining justice and order in a community. Similarly, a mature United Nations could, as envisioned by its original charter, exercise police power in behalf of the global community. Such exceptions to an absolutist pacifism are hinted at here and there in Muelder's writings.

Having made these points, I want to say that a very strong moral case can be made for such a modified form of pacifism. When one sees the deepening cycles of violence in the new 21st century world, with their awful human consequences, one is at least almost persuaded. One of the effects of the Iraq War, which was itself a monumental presidential blunder, has been a vivid demonstration of what lethal violence does to real people: death and bereavement, of course, but also loss of limbs, faces blown away, brains damaged, promising young lives ruined. Americans have had a vivid moment of truth. Consequences for innocent Iraqis of all ages have been on an even greater scale. Could nonviolent alternatives possibly be any worse?

We do know that nonviolent alternatives have worked in two 20th century situations where reasonable people had predicted blood baths: the struggle against racial segregation in the United States and against *apartheid* in South Africa. In both cases, courageous and imaginative leadership, committed to love and justice, proved able to minimize suffering, to overcome hostility, and to establish a much more humane and just social order. No social order is perfect, but the American South and South Africa could still be locked in desperate bloodshed if the racially oppressed in those countries had chosen the methods of violence. In both situations, the methods of nonviolence had deeply religious roots.

By contrast, conflicts in Northern Ireland, the Balkans, and the Middle East have been conducted violently for years, even for centuries. These unhappy situations have demonstrated how one round of violence can lead to another. It would appear that the thirst for vengeance can never be sufficiently sated. As I write, the Irish situation has come much closer to resolution, and there have been some hopeful accommodations in the Balkans. The Middle East remains seemingly intractable. Is pacifism, in some modified form, the elusive answer?

To move this question beyond the immediate historical frame of reference, we must take note of Muelder's criticism of Reinhold Niebuhr. Niebuhr had been a major figure in the leading American pacifist organization, the Fellowship of Reconciliation. But during the period leading up to World War II, Niebuhr abandoned that position and urged American intervention in behalf of England, even before Pearl Harbor. He had concluded that the evils of Hitler's Nazism could only be confronted militarily. That conclusion, and other historical observations, helped frame Niebuhr's theological response: the human propensity toward sin is too great for us to be able to rely upon nonviolence alone. If we are serious about the quest for justice on earth, we had better be prepared to fight for it.

With that background, the issue between Niebuhr and Muelder can be put simply: How much can we rely upon the goodness in human nature and the redemptive powers of God's grace in our struggle to overcome evil? Muelder understood the reality of sin. It was a question of how sinful is human nature and how perfectable? The differences between Muelder and Niebuhr on this point are relative. Muelder accepts the reality of sin and the need for institutional structures to undergird justice and protect the weak. Niebuhr acknowledges the human capacity for goodness in his famous aphorism: "Man's capacity for justice makes democracy possible; but man's inclination to injustice makes democracy necessary" (Preface, *The Children of Light and the Children of Darkness*).

Niebuhr's understanding of the Christian doctrine of original sin is classic, with its basis in the deep insecurity that is common to us all apart from faith in a power of love beyond us. Perhaps that is the very point where Muelder's greater confidence in the redemptive power of God is a correction to Niebuhr. Despite the realities of sin, God is also at work toward the redemption of our humanity. Is that power sufficient to sustain the pacifist commitment? Probably not in the absolutist sense, but then we have already observed that Muelder did not seem to have been an absolute pacifist. There may be, in his thought, some room for structures to undergird social justice, with the possibility of coercive sanctions when necessary. Here the ecumenical concept of the Responsible Society, so basic to Muelder, can protect our thinking about such needful structures from a too-ready disposition to use the short-cuts of violence. For those short-cuts have so often proved to be tragic detours in the quest for justice with peace.

After all, even the just war tradition has been insistent that violence should always be a last resort and that it should be responsible to a legitimate community. Muelder's form of pacifism can at least insist that any use of coercive violence should *be* a "last resort."

The Global Situation Beyond Muelder

Such discussions can remain on such an abstract level until the commitment to love and justice is creatively engaged with current realities. As we have seen, right up until his death Muelder was engaged. But he died in June, 2004, before the full tragedy of the Middle East had unfolded. What can one *now* say about the redemptive power of love, in this caldron of religious and ethnic hostilities, conducted with suicide bombing of marketplaces and mosques and utter disregard for the incontestable innocence of so many victims? And what of the torturing of prisoners, in disregard for the minimal standards of the Geneva Conventions? And the uses of high-tech modes of killing and maiming, conducted by a nation priding itself on civilized values?

It is not a stretch to say that the fundamental problem facing humanity today is religious in character. So many of the conflicts are between and even within religious communities. Perhaps that is one reason for the intensity of the conflicts and a predisposition to justify even the most violent means to achieve what are considered to be religiously required ends. Fanaticism is not limited to any one religion; it is arguable, indeed, that all of the world's great religions have given rise to fanaticism among all too many of their adherents. What can heal the madness?

While the problem may be essentially religious, it is more than doubtful that the faithful of any of the world's religions could convert the rest, thus establishing global spiritual unity and peace. But I wonder whether the kind of refined personalism that Muelder represents might have possibilities. Boiled down, this could mean commitments to love and humility. Both love and humility are expressed within the great religions, not by everybody and not all of the time, but nevertheless as a point of reference to which people can be recalled. Religious love acknowledges the oneness of humanity. Humility recognizes that ultimate reality, or God, is incomprehensibly bigger than any of us. I confess I do not know how love and humility could come to be at the heart of an emerging world culture that could become global community. At its best, that is the kind of vision that Muelder was devoted to, and it is worthy of our unstinting effort. *vs. romantic love*

Beyond Moral Humanism

But even that vision of communitarian personalism is not yet enough. It may be understandable that people would value a people-centered world, even a people-centered universe. Karl Barth, whose unacknowledged philosophical grounding was arguably personalist, developed a theology of creation that conceived of the physical, tangible aspects of reality as the basis and precondition of the covenant. The covenant, understood to be the meaning of creation, is to be understood as the divine-human relationship. Creation, in this view, is instrumental. The value of the covenant, by contrast, is intrinsic. Covenant is a good in and of itself. Creation is a good because it enables the covenant. Sometimes personalism came across a bit like that; Brightman in fact wrote insightfully about the contrast between intrinsic and instrumental values—the latter are valued because they help us to realize the former.

But the more recent ecological movement has helped us to see that there is more to the universe than the human. We are central to ourselves, but it is a bit of a leap to characterize the universe itself as anthropocentric. How are we to understand the rest of creation? One promising approach is suggested by the language of the first chapter of Genesis. In this beautiful myth, an aspect of creation occurred on each of the first six days, following which God rested. After several of the works of creation had been finished, God is depicted as seeing that it was good. So aspects of creation, preceding the creation of the first human beings, were seen by God as good. Good, that is, even before they were found to be useful by humankind. One might say that God *enjoyed* creation.

The rest of creation surely did become, in Barth's phrase, the basis and precondition of the covenant. But one might surely add that God, having taken pleasure in this work of creation, invited humankind to enjoy it as well. So the wonders of the universe, whether near at hand or far away, are to be taken as good as they are found to be good by God. A part of the meaning of the covenant, then, is our sharing this good, this pleasure, with God. This does not detract from the personalistic vision; it gives that vision greater enrichment.

It seems pointless for Christians to try to convert all the Buddhists, Muslims, Hindus, and Jews (etc.) on earth-and vice-versa, for any of them to seek to convert Christians. But might there be something in this broader vision of appreciation for the beauty and wonder of being that could touch all of us in new ways? And might we not all see with fresh eyes the importance of protecting this treasure far into the future?

Sharing the planet —

—JPW

About the Editor

After completing his Ph.D. with Walter Muelder in 1960, J. Philip Wogaman taught at University of the Pacific and then for 26 years (11 as dean) at Wesley Theological Seminary. An internationally recognized scholar in Christian ethics, Wogaman has written or edited some 20 books. Other published writings have appeared in scores of books, journals and magazines, including *The Progressive Christian* where his column on ethics appears regularly. He is past president of the American Theological Society, the Society of Christian Ethics, and the national Interfaith Alliance. From 1992 to 2002 he was Senior Minister of Foundry United Methodist Church in Washington, DC attended by the Clintons and other national leaders. In 2004 he was called out of retirement to serve for two years as Interim President of the Iliff School of Theology. Wogaman lives with Carolyn, his wife of 50 years, in Washington, DC.